Meredith Willson

The Unsinkable Music Man

John C. Skipper

Savas Publishing Company

Manufactured in the United States of America

Meredith Willson: The Unsinkable Music Man
John C. Skipper

Includes bibliographic references and index

Printing Number
10 9 8 7 6 5 4 3 2 1
First Edition

ISBN 1-882810-78-3 (paper)
ISBN 1-882810-05-8 (cloth)

Savas Publishing Company
202 First Street SE, Suite 103A
Mason City, IA 50401

(641) 421-7135 (editorial offices)
(800) 732-3669 (distribution)

This book is printed on acid-free paper. It meets or exceeds the guidelines for permanence and durability of the Committee on Production Guidelines for Book Longevity of the Council on Library Resources

For Sandi, Suzanne and Jennifer Skipper
and Dennis, Stephanie and Andrew Clark

May the Good Lord Bless and Keep You

Robert Meredith Willson

Table of Contents

continued. . .

Table of Contents (continued)

Photos and Illustrations

continued. . .

Photos and Illustrations *(continued)*

The Long Journey

He was pretty adamant about it.

"No! Absolutely not!"

By this time the man sitting in the chair across from my desk was holding his hands up in front of him like two fleshy stop signs. "Ted, I am still finishing a book for another publisher, and *that* deadline is coming up soon."

Utilizing a talent that took me years to perfect (and I still find difficult to implement), I leaned back slowly and kept my mouth closed. My gaze never left his face, but his eyes left mine.

"I am way too busy as it is. Besides, my wife would kill me if I took on a new project like this one." The man's jaw set even more firmly than before, but his voice betrayed otherwise. He was shaking his head, but he was also weakening. I could sense it.

"John," I began softly, my voice almost a whisper. I waited until he looked at me and then leaned forward, resting my elbows on the desktop. "I only tie my wagon to busy people. You are going to write this book. You just won't admit it yet."

Like just about every book ever written, *Meredith Willson: The Unsinkable Music Man* experienced an interesting genesis. After practicing law and running a publishing company in California for a dozen years, I moved my family back to my home town in 1998. Although we published military and general history books, it seemed logical to develop a local interest title. My marketing director at that time, Nancy Lund, suggested a pair of possibilities: Buddy Holly (who played his last concert here and was killed when his plane crashed)—and Meredith Willson. Buddy Holly did not immediately catch my fancy, but the latter suggestion intrigued me from the start.

Indeed, Willson seemed destined for a good book—especially since construction crews were beginning to break ground just down the street on The Music Man Square, and his boyhood home is open for tours. I thought carefully about the idea for several weeks and even considered potential authors for the project. In the end none of them, for a variety of reasons, were deemed suitable.

And then John Skipper walked into my office one day.

"Hi," he said, "I did an article on you and a Confederate submarine about five years ago, and thought I should stop in and say hello."

I knew John was a respected reporter for the *Mason City Globe Gazette*, and his friendliness, deep voice, and warm cheer were instantly infectious. What I did not know was that he was also the author of several baseball-related books. Sitting in my office surrounded by books and a wall plastered with dust jackets, the subject naturally came up.

"Baseball?"

"Yeah, baseball."

"Three books?"

He nodded his head proudly. "I am finishing my fourth one right now." He then proceeded to fill me in on the details of each title.

The more he spoke the more passionate and animated he became. By the time he finished, his blue-gray eyes were flashing with excitement. This man loved his work. And I love being around and working with passionate people.

"Are you concerned at all about being stereotyped as a baseball author?" I held my breath. His answer was important to me.

"Yes," he quickly replied. "I love baseball, but I love lots of other things, too." As it turned out, local history was one of them.

We talked for several minutes about his research, writing style, methodology, general interests, working with publishers and editors, and the book trade in general. By this time the mail had arrived, phones were ringing, and it was obvious to both of us that we had to get back to work. He had a deadline to meet with the *Globe Gazette*, and I had an author in North Carolina who needed a verbal kick in the pants.

As John walked out the door, he paused to shake my hand. "It's great meeting you. Who knows, maybe we will do a project together sometime." We both laughed. The thought had already crossed my mind. And I knew exactly what he was going to write.

A few days later John walked into my office to comment on a recent book we had released. "I am glad you are here," I said. "Come in and sit down, I have a project I want to run by you and need your opinion." Everybody likes to be asked for their opinion. He had no idea what was in store for him.

I pulled down a copy of *1912 Facts About Titanic,* one of our most popular books, and passed it over to him. "We developed this series, and I think a book similar to it on Meredith Willson would be great. He was an important fellow for a host of reasons, and it needs to be done. What do you think."

"That's a great idea!" His response was genuinely enthusiastic. "Especially with the 'Square' going up and all the interest about him and his music here."

He paused for a moment and then added, "You know, most of the archival material you would need is right here in town."

"Yes, I know."

"Pictures, too. Most of them are over in the library archives as well."

"Yup, they are just down the street," I answered.

"And make sure you speak with Art Fischbeck," John advised. "Do you know Art? He is Mason City's unofficial town historian. Art has forgotten more about this town and its history than most people will ever learn."

"Oh, sure, I know Art," I replied. "My mom and him have been friends for decades." There was a brief lull in the conversation as we both thought about the project.

"Of course, you have to find someone to write this," he stated matter-of-factly, "and that could be tough."

I leaned back and smiled. "Oh, I already have an author."

His expression changed immediately to one of surprise. "Really? Is it a local guy?" The reporter sitting in front of me thought he was going to get a scoop. John was visibly restraining himself from reaching for his pen and notepad.

"Yeah, he's local," I replied. "And well known, a good writer, lots of experience."

This time a long, pregnant silence followed. It was more than he could stand. It was almost more than I could stand.

"Well . . . who is it?" he asked.

I looked at him and smiled. And kept smiling. And that was when the conversation opening this preface took place.

A week later I bumped into John eating lunch with a friend at The Other Place, a local eatery just across the street from my office. He waved at me from the first booth inside the door and I strolled over to say hello. I directed my first words to his companion.

"Did John tell you about our new project?"

An audible groan erupted from the reporter as he bit down into a gigantic Iowa pork tenderloin sandwich, one of the OP's specialties. John shook his head and looked up at me over his glasses. "I have one project, and it is a *baseball* book!"

I walked over to the bar and paid for my pair of Cheese pizza slices and drink. It was another day of lunch over a desk. In the best Colombo tradition I could muster, I stopped and turned around just before reaching the door.

"Oh, one more thing," I added, looking at directly at John. "I am drafting a contract for you to read over before you begin researching Willson. Drop by when you get a chance and we can discuss it."

I will never forget the look of shock on his face as I walked out the door. I laughed so hard I dropped my ice tea on the sidewalk.

John called three days later. "Do you have a few minutes for lunch today?" We agreed to meet at the OP at noon.

"I have been thinking about this Willson project," he began. "I really am busy finishing this baseball book, but I spent a day over at the library archives thumbing through some of their Willson holdings. It is a gold mine over there . . ."

"I know," I replied. "I heard you were rummaging around and asking questions."

I opened the black folder I had been carrying and removed a contract. Within an hour we had agreed on terms, a tentative first draft manuscript deadline, and a working title.

John's enthusiasm for this project was evident from day one, and his fervor only grew as his research progressed. His days off from the paper were spent sitting in the west wing of the Mason City Public Library at a large wooden table covered with photos, manuscript material, and books. Since my office is just one block north, he often dropped by unannounced to fill me in on his latest find. They were welcomed interuptions. "Did you know that Meredith Willson . . ." was how his conversations invariably began.

Almost a year passed and one day the phone rang. It was John.

"I have something for you. Are you going to be in?" I knew what it was before he showed up with it.

The first thing I pulled from the manuscript to read was "Pioneers and Miracles," John's aptly titled and moving prologue. Before I knew it I had read the first four chapters without leaving my chair.

My own journey to discovering Meredith Willson covered a long and circuitous passage. No one will ever confuse me with the famous composer, but we did have at least one thing in common: both of us were fortunate to have mothers willing to instill within us a deep love and appreciation of music. Unfortunately for me, one of us was Wolfgang Mozart, and the other, Antonio Salieri.

John Skipper's descriptions of Meredith's years of hard work as a boy learning to play the piano, flute, and piccolo brought forth a flood of long forgotten memories of spending hours on a piano bench, a metronome ticking back and forth in an often vain attempt to keep me on beat. The years of lugging my clarinet and music stand the three blocks to Harding School also conjured up a smile. Yes, I could appreciate that aspect of Meredith's childhood.

In 1968, the local community theater put on *The Music Man*. I was only nine years old, but even I understood this was a big thing for Mason City. Everyone wanted to play a part. At my mother's urging I stood in my living room for hours singing "Gary, Indiana" and practicing a lisp in the hope of winning the coveted role of Winthrop. After a couple of auditions the dozen or so hopefuls had been whittled down to just me and another kid. I lost the role on a warm and sunny Saturday afternoon after the last of several call backs. I still remember the keen disappointment I felt when my mom told me I would not get the part. I think she felt even worse than I did.

In the end, my participation consisted of a role as an extra and usher. At that time the name Meredith Willson did not mean much to me, but I still remember escorting he and his new wife Rosemary to their seats. My little sister had the honor of presenting Rosemary with a bouquet of roses. All in all, it was a grand time that I will always remember fondly.

Ten years later I was dating the granddaughter of Art Swanson, Meredith Willson's boyhood pal and lifelong friend. I may have even met Meredith on one of his trips home during this period of my life because he often ate dinner with the Swansons. But I was a young high school graduate then, and so wrapped up in myself that I honestly don't remember for sure whether I did or not. I do recall hearing an earful about the musician from Tom Swanson, Art's son. "Yes, I know he wrote a song recorded by the Beatles," I said over and over. There was no way I was going to act impressed in front of my girlfriend's dad—even if I was.

And then my life came full circle on the subject, as life often has a way of doing. Now, on the wrong side of forty, I am editing and publishing a book about the man, his life, and his wonderful music. It is the most enjoyable project I have ever had the pleasure of working on.

I finished John's first draft of the manuscript sitting at my kitchen table long hours after sleep had overtaken my wife and kids. I found it to be an uplifting story of one man's struggle to achieve success against long odds. The boy who left Mason City on a train for New York with nothing but a few dollars in his pocket and a bent piccolo had realized his life's ambition—and then some. It is a true story of the proverbial "hometown boy" who leaves for stardom and fortune, but never forgets his roots and his friends.

And then it suddenly dawned on me. A wave of sadness washed through me that lingers still: I had lost a friend I never knew I had. Willson had been around me my whole life in so many ways, and it took four decades and an accidental meeting with John Skipper for me to realize it.

I hope readers of *Meredith Willson: The Unsinkable Music Man* figure it out sooner than I did.

Theodore P. Savas
Mason City, Iowa

September 1, 2000

Willson has two "ls"

hen I came to work for the *Mason City Globe-Gazette* on July 21, 1986, my co-workers offered the usual greetings and well-wishes that newcomers always get on their first day on a new job. Jim Owens, who had been at the paper in various capacities for about 30 years and then was in charge of the editorial page, offered something a little different. He approached my desk with gray moustache twitching a little and his glasses slipping down the bridge of his nose as he leaned over to offer his greeting. "MacNider is 'Mac' and Willson has two 'ls.' Remember those two things and you'll be fine," he said.

MacNider is the name of a well-to-do Mason City family that for several generations had donated generously to the community and continues to do so. As for Willson—he was a hometown boy who had left to seek fame and fortune and made good. Being from Oak Park, Illinois, I was familiar with that storyline. I came of age on the same street, Kenilworth Avenue, where Ernest Hemingway grew up. Hemingway left Oak Park when he was 18 and pretty well forgot about the place, and for years the community recognized the snub and resented it.

Just the opposite occurred in Mason City. Willson, like Hemingway, left his hometown as a teenager (Willson was only 17 when he headed for New York)—but never forgot his roots. And the community appreciated his lifelong support and responded in kind. I arrived in Mason City two years after Willson's death, but Owens' sage advice on my first day at work was testimony to how Willson was gone but not forgotten.

Meredith Willson raced into the hearts of music lovers in 1957 when *The Music Man* began a run of 1,375 performances on Broadway and the stirring "*Seventy-Six Trombones*" became one of the great American marches. Before making it big on Broadway, he spent three decades in radio, where he served as the musical director for NBC and appeared on many programs. Whenever he got the chance, he mentioned his hometown on the air. In its listing of radio programs, the local newspaper, the *Mason City Globe Gazette*, with unabashed pride labeled one particular show "The Meredith Willson Hour." In fact, Willson did not have a show; instead, he led the orchestra on a show whose name should have been listed for that time slot.

When I was approached about writing a biography of Meredith Willson, two aspects of the project seemed particularly intriguing. First, no biography of Willson had ever been published. The second and most challenging aspect would be to research and write a book that got beyond the man's legend and told his real life story—and lets the chips fall where they may.

As it turns out, they didn't fall far from the table. In fact, my research largely supports the legend. The result is *Meredith Willson: The Unsinkable Music Man*. It tells an amazing story of how a youngster with talent and tenacity, possessed with what he would later call a streak of "Iowa stubborn," rose to become one of America's most famous musicians. He struggled hard to achieve his dreams, and like most successful careers in any field, he had to work to overcome many bumps along the way—in both his personal and professional life. Accounts of these trials and triumphs are included in this work, warts and all, for they are as much a part of his life as the bumps in our roads are part of ours.

Every effort has been made to tell Willson's story in his own words through the examination of hundreds of his newspaper and magazine interviews spanning 60 years, as well as tapes of radio broadcasts and concert appearances, and his five books. I also relied on interviews with people who knew him, and was thus able to assess both the public and private man.

But this is not intended to be the definitive and all-inclusive story of Willson's life. It is instead one man's account of another man's time on this earth. Every effort has been made to show what forces shaped Willson's life, factors such as personality, parental influence, siblings, friends, school, church, romance, grit, and in some cases, dumb luck.

In order to be successful, any research project of this scope and magnitude is absolutely dependent on two factors: the trail that is left by those in the past whose writings and broadcasts of events in their day now serve as the meat and potatoes for the next generation of researchers; and the cooperation of many people who believe in the project and offer their time and help without asking anything in return. Indeed, their reward is my heartfelt thanks and the belief that they can take pride in the final product, hopefully knowing it wouldn't have happened without their contribution.

Art Fischbeck, Mason City's historian, offered me support and encouragement all along the way, read a draft of the manuscript, and offered editing suggestions. A researcher becomes a historian when he is able to take a set of isolated facts and connect the dots, and nobody does it better than Art.

Andrew Alexander, director of the Mason City, Iowa, public library and Terry Harrison, archivist, provided me with access to important documents and photographs, offered suggestions, and were always of good cheer. Their cooperation, advice, encouragement, and patience with me were an immense help in seeing this project through to completion.

Special thanks go to Theodore P. Savas, owner of Savas Publishing Company, who developed an idea for a book and who should write it—and then would not take "no" for an answer. I am indebted to him not only for his support and encouragement, but most important, for his confidence in me. Carol Savas read an early draft of the manuscript and offered several helpful suggestions that, in the end, made this a better book.

Others whose contributions are greatly appreciated include: Dan Bjerke, Cliff Carlson, Lenore Clifford, Jim Collison, Val Collison, Ted Enabnit, Eric Endres, Don Freeman, Al Heinz, Jeff Heinz, Dee Leaman, Jack Leaman, Sandy Lee, Mark Lemon, Gil Lettow, Carl Miller, Don Morrison, Phyllis Morrison, Deb Nicklay, Howard Query, Jennifer Skipper, John Smalley, the Rev. Robert Stone, Ann Swanson and Tom Swanson, Charles Walk, and John Vance Jr.

And the greatest living resource of all, Rosemary Willson.

Many others too numerous to mention also helped me in one way or another. You know who you are, and I am indebted to your assistance.

The biggest thanks, as always, goes to Sandi Skipper. Without her love and understanding, none of this would have been possible.

John C. Skipper
Mason City, Iowa

August 9, 2000

Prologue

Pioneers and Miracles

A lively crowd gathered around the grand piano in the Hotel Hanford on a warm June evening in 1962. The Hanford was the finest hotel in Mason City, Iowa, and, at eight stories, the tallest building in this city of 30,000, or in all of Cerro Gordo County for that matter. Mason City is situated almost exactly halfway between Des Moines, Iowa, and Minneapolis, Minnesota, and is surrounded by an area where barns and silos are more prominent than bricks and mortar.

The Hanford was a showplace, a convention center in corn country, and when there was a major event happening in Mason City, it was happening at the Hanford. The man sitting at the piano was in the hotel's Euchre and Cycle Club on the top floor of the hotel, a setting that had hosted some of Mason City's finest parties over the years. He played one song after another, sometimes singing, sometimes talking his way through the songs, with friends gathered around him, many placing their hands on the piano as they sang along, tapping their fingers and lifting them only long enough to clap as one song ended and another began.

Someone once said that "you can't go home again." Perhaps. But Meredith Willson, the man at the piano, had not only come home again to his beloved Mason City—the hometown that he mentioned so often on his radio and television broadcasts—but he had brought some of Hollywood with him. Robert Preston, the great stage and screen star was seated close by, as was Shirley Jones, winner of the 1960 Academy Award for her role as best supporting actress in *Elmer Gantry*. They were now the stars of Willson's new movie *The Music Man*.

The Music Man was Preston's 38th motion picture. He landed the movie role after Willson watched his electrified performances on Broadway, where *The Music Man* played for almost four years with Preston in the lead role. Jones was equally famous, not only for her Oscar-winning performance but also for roles in other hit musicals, such as *Oklahoma!* and *Carousel*. She would later win acclaim as the matriarch on *The Partridge Family*, a popular 1970s television program. Even young Ronnie Howard had made the trip to Mason City. The precocious eight-year-old was already nationally famous as "Opie" on the Andy Griffith television program. Years later he would appear as Richie Cunningham on the TV's *Happy Days*, and would go on to become a successful film producer and director. But on that June evening in 1962, he was a little boy who movie-goers would remember as Winthrop, the lad with the lisp who sang about "Gary, Indiana." Radio and TV personality Arthur Godfrey, whose red hair and freckles belied his middle-aged years, was also in town.

They were all in Mason City to witness Willson's greatest tribute to his birthplace: the film version of *The Music Man* was about to premiere in his home town. Godfrey hosted one of the most popular radio programs in America from 1945 to 1972, and had two high-rated television programs in the 1950s. He was the Oprah Winfrey of his time, with his folksy banter and ability to book big-name guests. But Godfrey did not have a role in the movie. Willson brought him to town to serve as the public address announcer on opening night, to officially announce the guests as they arrived at the Palace Theater.

All of these stars were in Mason City to honor Willson or, more accurately, to help Willson honor his home town. The *Mason City Globe-Gazette* was covering all of the activities, of course, just as it had tracked its favorite son's career since he was a teenager. And KGLO radio and television were each providing coverage for the local residents. But other media came to town as well, from Des Moines and Cedar Rapids, from Minneapolis—and from Hollywood. Such was the drawing power of Meredith Willson.

The Music Man had not come easy for the man whose talent and volume of music made it seem like everything came easy. Willson had been asked many times to write a musical about Iowa, and had always declined, deeming other projects more suitable. When people stopped asking, he began wondering whether others thought he couldn't do it. One of the reasons he wrote *The Music Man*, by his own admission, was to prove that

Morton Da Costa, director of *The Music Man*, holds young Ronnie Howard in his lap as he talks during a party at the Hotel Hanford in Mason City after the movie premiere. Flanking him are the movie's stars, Shirley Jones and Robert Preston. Meredith Willson is enjoying the moment at far right. *MCPLA*

he could. And it took him five long years and dozens of rewrites to perfect it.

By the time he and his friends gathered at the Hotel Hanford in June of 1962, Willson had nothing to prove. He looked up from the piano every so often to flash his broad smile, his dark-horned rimmed glasses and full head of brown hair, with a bit of a wave in it, were part of his persona. Sometimes his hair would be askew as he bobbed his head back and forth while he played or conducted. Tonight, he simply played and sang. And the people sang with him, one song after another, from the great Broadway hit that was about to be a major motion picture.

One man in the room tried to move around to get a good look at the back of Willson's head. Clifford Carlson, a sculptor from the neighboring Iowa town of Wesley, had been commissioned to do a statue of the famed musician. So to him, the back of Willson's head was as important as the front. As he maneuvered to get the best view, he marveled at the subject of his work. "Meredith sat down at the piano. We all gathered around, standing up close, our hands on the top of that grand piano, as he played, sang and talked his way through the entire creation of *The Music Man*—song by song, scene by scene," remembered Carlson.

The songs included the vocal "chug, chug, chug" of the train on its way to "River City, Ioway," the simple honesty of "Iowa Stubborn," the uplifting strains of "Wells Fargo Wagon," the triumphant "76 Trombones," and the loveliest of love songs, "Til There Was You." According to the Wesley sculptor, "There was no vain bragging —not even a hint, just that wonderful exuberance of creativity. It was a glorious experience, standing there looking into the very soul of this man as he once again relived *The Music Man* and gloried in sharing it with old friends back home."

Carlson, who died before he completed his work, fretted about the challenge of doing justice to his famous subject. "A sculptor has only two silent hands and a lump of clay with which to speak. In order to speak loudly and clearly, things must be condensed, all non-essentials weeded out and everything brought into focus," he said.

The focus on the life of Meredith Willson passes through much more than New York and Hollywood, much more than stage and screen, radio and television. It strikes his youthful adventures growing up in a family with parents who implored their children to be daring; his days in John Philip Sousa's band, and playing under the baton of the great Arturo Toscanini; and his assistance in helping create sound for motion pictures and in writing the music for Charlie Chaplin's first "talkie." It touches his work as the youngest conductor of the San Francisco Symphony Orchestra, and on his successful radio career, his association with George Burns, Gracie Allen, and Tallulah Bankhead, and his participation in the early days of television. It shines on *The Music Man* and *The Unsinkable Molly Brown*, and the writing of such musical classics as "May The Good Lord Bless and Keep You," and "It's Beginning to Look Like Christmas."

In so many ways Meredith Willson's life is an American classic, the "small town boy makes good" story. The teenager who left Mason City, Iowa, on a train bound for New York in search of a career, carrying with him only a few dollars and a bent piccolo. It is a story with more ups than downs, more accomplishments than failures, more good fortune than misfortune. In order to capture the essence of the man, to grasp what Carlson sought to depict in his sculpture as he watched Meredith Willson sitting at the piano on that June night in 1962, one must travel only about two blocks from the Hotel Hanford to the First Congregational Church. There, 60 years earlier, Rosalie Willson, Meredith's mother, directed the Sunday School for 32 years. A few blocks to the south, she and her husband raised their three children at 314 S. Superior (today's Pennsylvania) Avenue. Dixie, the couple's oldest child, would grow up to be a famous author, poet, and screenwriter. Cedric was destined to become one of the nation's great civil engineers. And then there was Meredith, the boy who was always fascinated with music.

Hazel Griffith Erwin, Meredith's childhood friend, later recalled that when Willson went to New York at the age of 17 and eventually landed a job with the Sousa band, a woman struck up a conversation in Mason City with his Aunt Mae, whom she did not realize was a relative. "I hear that Willson boy is traveling with Sousa's band. I'm glad our children are normal," she said.

John and Rosalie Willson raised their children to strive for excellence. Meredith recalled his father bidding him farewell when the son was about to board the train for New York. "Meredith," he said, "I want to tell you a little something about America, and that includes New York. It is a land of challenges and a country of pioneers, whether you be a musician or a homesteader. What I am trying to say is this: Folks warm-heartedly applaud any man who breaks new ground or attains new heights, whether he be a Rockefeller or just a boy like yourself. But you've got to work hard for it. It's there to be had. You know, son, you sorta gotta be a pioneer." That, at least, is how Meredith remembered the conversation. It is likely that he incorporated some of his own language into the retelling, since "sorta" is not a phrase John Willson would have used. But "pioneer" is.

Many of Rosalie Willson's Sunday School children stayed in touch with her. It was common for high school students to come to the Willson home to talk to her about their futures. She gave many of them a card inscribed with the following quotation from author Philip Brooks:

> Do not pray for easy lives. Pray to be stronger men. Do not pray for tasks equal to your powers. Pray for power equal to your tasks. Then the doing of your work shall be no miracle, but you shall be the miracle. Everyday you shall wonder at yourself, at the richness of your life, which has come to you by the grace of God.

Pioneers and miracles. Such were the goals and dreams laid out in the fabric of family philosophy John and Rosalie Willson wove for their children. They groomed their children for greatness. For Meredith, the essence of what his parents had dreamed for him, the essence of what he had dreamed of, and what he had come to be, was embodied in the music and the people around the piano in the Hotel Hanford almost a half-century later.

Once again, he had pulled it off. Meredith Willson had come home.

Chapter 1

"Mama's doing."

— *Meredith Willson*

Prayers and Banjos

When Robert Meredith Willson entered the world on May 18, 1902, at 14 pounds, 6 ounces, he was the largest baby ever born in Iowa. As he grew up, he strove to be the best at everything he did. Performing was in his blood from an early age.

When he wasn't participating in one of his mother's church presentations, Meredith was often engaged in an impromptu production he, his mother, his sister Dixie, and brother Cedric had dreamt up in their front yard or in the family living room of their roomy two-story frame house on Superior Avenue. Rosalie encouraged her children to perform for others. Indeed, it was an unwritten Willson household mandate. For Meredith, it was just a way to have a lot of fun.

The young Meredith was born full of dreams and inspirations. As a youngster, he would lie awake in bed at night, listening to the train whistles blow in the stillness of Iowa after dark. One day, he believed, he would be on that train, traveling to one gig or another. By the time he reached high school, Meredith played a mean flute and was setting his sights on performing in the band of the great John Philip Sousa.

The Willson roots for adventure and striving for excellence ran several generations deep. When John Willson talked to Meredith about the importance of being a pioneer, he had only to look to his own father, Alonzo Willson, as an example. Alonzo Willson, Meredith's grandfather, was born in Adams Center, New York, on July 21, 1822. The family left New York in 1836 and moved to Illinois, where Alonzo married Catherine Reynolds on February 2, 1845. Alonzo and his family tried their hand at farming in Illinois, where settlers occasionally fought Blackhawk Indians—or "bloody savages" as Alonzo called them. The restless Willson spirit, however, left Alonzo unsatisfied and searching for something more.

About this time he began hearing tales of men who had traveled west and returned home with vast riches. Miners had struck gold in California, and anyone willing to work hard could make a fortune there. Or so the rumors went. Unable to resist the temptation, in 1853 Alonzo organized a team of about 40 men, some of whom brought their families with them, and headed west on horseback. Occasionally, he said, they encountered Indians

Alonzo Willson and his wife, Catherine, had a pioneer spirit that carried on through three generations of the Willson family. *MCPLA*

but, in Willson's words, he and his party "worsted" them and continued on their way.

The entourage disbanded in Marysville, California, and Alonzo rode off to seek his fortune. When he returned to Iowa two years later, he had amassed about $10,000—not in nugget gold, however, but in cash from deals he had made with the gold miners. He moved his family from Illinois to Cerro Gordo County, Iowa. The wealthiest land owner there was Anson C. Owen, who owned all the timberland in an area known locally as Owen's Grove a few miles southeast of present-day Mason City. Owen approached Willson and inquired whether he wanted to purchase some of the adjoining land so that he could farm. Willson, who had proven his worth as a businessman in California, worked out a deal and wound up owning much of Owen's Grove. Later, he set up a business and loaned money to farmers, who put up their land as collateral. Within a few years, he was one of the wealthiest men in the county and held vast land holdings.

Alonzo oversaw construction of the first school in the township and served as its first teacher. He also established the first public library and served as justice of the peace. He was indeed a pioneer in many ways, and paved the way for two generations of his family to strive to not only be the best, but be the first.

Alonzo fathered eight children, five of whom, Emma, Alice, Bruce, B.B. and Lenora ("Norrie"), were born in New York. Mae, Gertrude, and John were all born in Iowa. (Mae is the "Aunt Mae" who heard the stranger say she was glad she had "normal" children who weren't like young Meredith Willson.) The result of the wide difference in ages of Alonzo Willson's family is that John Willson had a sister, Emma, old enough to be his mother.

John Willson, Meredith's father, was born August 4, 1866, on his father's farm in Owen's Grove. The family moved to Mason City in 1878. (The city's original name was Shibboleth. Alonzo Willson was one of the citizens who came up with its present name.) John Willson would have been in the graduating class of 1883 at Mason City High School, but there were only six members that year. As a result, the board of education decided to retain the class for an additional year. Willson and his five classmates protested and quit school. The following year, he enrolled in a two-year law course at the University of Notre Dame. Upon completion, he traveled to Indianapolis to take the state bar association examination. There, John stood before state supreme court justices and lied under oath so that he could take the test to practice law. The minimum legal age to practice law was 21; John was only 18.

After passing the bar, John practiced law for one year in Zenith, Kansas, before moving to Estherville, Iowa, where he once again hung out his shingle. The legal technicalities of day-to-day lawyering bored him, however, and John decided to try something else. He tried his hand at banking in Estherville, but that profession was similarly unfulfilling. Before long he found an interest in real estate and real estate development. Like his father had done many years earlier in Owen Township, John Willson built the first brick building in Estherville. Eventually, the family moved to Mason City, where he managed his father's real estate holdings and dabbled in other business ventures, even owning a bakery for a few years.

During his tenure at Notre Dame, John played on the school baseball team. On a road trip to Chicago he met Rosalie Reiniger, a Brighton, Illinois, school teacher six years older than himself. Rosalie was a native of Charles City, Iowa, the daughter of Gustavus G. Reiniger, a prominent lawyer, and Lida Meacham. When Rosalie was five, her family moved to Union, Missouri, where her father took a seat as a district judge. When he died three years later, Lida moved her family to Brighton, where Rosalie spent the rest of her childhood.

Rosalie had aspirations of being a teacher, and in 1885 graduated from the Kindergarten course at Armour Institute in Chicago. In 1888, she graduated from the Kindergarten Department at Iowa State Teachers College (known today as the University of Northern Iowa) at Cedar Falls. She was ready to embark on a career that would shape the rest of her life—teaching young children right from wrong and helping them progress to the next level of their learning.

While attending the Armour Institute, Rosalie went to a ball game in Chicago and met a Notre Dame ballplayer named John Willson. The pair courted and eventually married on August 28, 1889, at the Congregational church in Brighton. They made their home in Estherville before moving to Mason City two years later. Mrs. Willson quickly put her education to good use: she started the first kindergarten in Mason City, and was superintendent of the primary department of the First Congregational Church for 32 years. She and her husband also started a family.

The Willsons had six children. The eldest was Lucille Reiniger Willson, born on August 6, 1890. Lucille is better known by her nickname, "Dixie," which followed her until the end of her life. A second daughter, Maurine,

John and Rosalie Willson in Estherville, Iowa, early in their marriage. It is not known what book John is holding. Dixie Willson said her parents mentally programmed the occupations of their three children, an idea John got from a book he read. *MCPLA*

was born four years later, but tragedy struck when she contracted spinal meningitis at the age of five months and five days, and died on October 5, 1894. John Cedrick Willson was born on October 26, 1900. To the Willsons and his friends, he was known simply as Cedric. The Willson's fourth child, Robert Meredith Willson, was born on May 18, 1902. Almost nothing is

Rosalie enjoying a quiet moment with her three children in their
home on Superior Avenue. Meredith is sitting on her lap. *MCPLA*

know of the other two offspring. Whether they died in infancy or were late
term miscarriages is unknown.

Meredith often expressed fond memories of his boyhood days growing
up in the house that was once part of his grandfather's real estate holdings.
The house now belonged to his parents, who Meredith always called
"Mama" and "Papa."

It was a three-story (including an attic) frame affair that was full of life
and charm. It was not unusual for Rosalie, in the company of Cedric and
Meredith, to organize neighborhood children for a little skit on the first
floor or on the spacious front porch while Dixie was in the attic, sitting at a

little desk in front of a window that looked out over her backyard and beyond. It was from there that Dixie composed her poems and short stories, a labor of love that was also the first inkling of what would grow to become a lifelong career. The desk had once been in her bedroom. In later years, she had fond memories of writing in both places.

The first floor of the home had a large living room, dining room, and kitchen. Large double doors leading into a parlor at the front of the home separated it from the living room. It was in that kitchen and dining room that Meredith developed his infamous—and lifelong—love of pies. The boys were introduced to music on an old upright piano in the parlor. John Willson's guitar was often found propped up against the wall next to the piano. The parlor was also a place for quiet solitude for either of the parents. When the parlor doors were closed, the children knew better than to enter without knocking, lest the peaceful moment be shattered.

The second floor of the Superior Avenue home had a nursery at the top of the stairs on the right, and a master bedroom (where Meredith was born) on the left. Down a narrow hallway was Dixie's bedroom and another room shared by Cedric and Meredith. The house had a large, open front porch that often served as the setting for some of Rosalie's kindergarten classes. The porch was enclosed when Meredith was about ten.

There were two unmistakable sounds associated with the Willson house: the sound of music flowing from the piano in the parlor, or later, from Meredith's flute, Cedric's bassoon, or Dixie's harp; and the sound of scampering feet on the hardwood floors of the second floor as Cedric and Meredith sauntered up and down the hall, from the stairway to their back bedroom.

Like just about every household, the Willsons followed certain established rituals. Monday night, for example, was cribbage night for Papa and Dixie. Meredith said he grew up hearing phrases from those cribbage games like "fifteen-two, fifteen-four, fifteen-six and a pair is eight," and was never curious as to what it meant. Tuesday nights were set aside for band and orchestra rehearsals—on alternating Tuesdays—because that was the night that seemed to work out best for the participants. Wednesday was church night and choir practice. Thursday night was set aside for Christian Endeavor, a religious education training. Friday evenings usually meant a family trip to the Star Theatre, where the Willsons would watch the latest available entertainment. Saturday night was a time for the children to do something with Mama, and trips to the library were not uncommon. Sundays were set aside for attending church three times in the same day, or as Meredith recalled it, once in the morning, once in the evening, and

Rosalie Willson started the first kindergarten in Cerro Gordo County, Iowa. It often met on the front porch of the Willson family home. In upper photo, some of the children are in costume. There were few things Mrs. Willson loved more than teaching children. *MCPLA*

Sunday school. (He counted Sunday School as a third time even though it was part of the Sunday morning going-to-church activity.)

According to Meredith, many of the activities of the Willson children in their formative years were "Mama's doing." Dixie agreed. "In Mason City, mother's only outlet . . . was with the children." After Meredith learned to play the piano, she encouraged him to master another instrument—so he would stand out from the other boys in school. Meredith chose the flute. She read aloud every night to Cedric and Meredith from a book called *What Every Boy Should Know*, a dry etiquette manual about how to act when in the company of the opposite sex.

When Rosalie Willson believed in something, she was relentless in her efforts to bring others along. She was described as "a very religious woman" by some, "a sanctimonious old gal" by others. It was not unusual for Rosalie to adorn the walls, mirrors, and doors of the Willson home with banners, notes, and signs conveying little messages to passers-by. "God Gave You This Day: Meet the Challenge" was posted on the bathroom mirror; "Remember, Do Unto Others. . ." hung from the door leading outside the home.

Rosalie was a kind woman and a loving mother. She also possessed a sternness and a deep sense of propriety that showed in almost everything she did, particularly in how she handled children—her own, her kindergartners, and her Sunday School students. She never scolded a child by saying something like "how could you do such a thing?" preferring instead to politely point out the child's error. She insisted that her children always refer to women by name in conversation, rather than using the word "she," no matter how many times the name was mentioned in the same conversation.

Sometimes, her delicate balancing act between kindness and propriety stretched her to her limits. One day in Sunday School, she was delivering the lesson about Jesus being out in the desert for 40 days and 40 nights. One of the students who listened intently was a little boy with a terrible lisp. "What would be the first thing you would do when you got home after being gone that long?" she asked her class. The little boy thought a moment, and then blurted out, "Pith." Without visible reaction, Rosalie continued on with the lesson.

When Sunday School was over she bid each of her students goodbye, walked home briskly, went into a little room off the living room, and closed the door. When Meredith arrived a few moments later, he heard strange noises coming from the room. He knew better than to enter when the door was closed. He shouted to his father to check on Mama. John Willson opened the door and found his wife sitting in her favorite chair, doubled up with the laughter she had stifled the entire time it took her to end Sunday School and walk home.

In addition to her kindergarten classes at the church, Rosalie conducted informal classes in her home that attracted children from all over the neighborhood. A few years later, when she saw some of these same children walking home from school or playing in the neighborhood, she would stop and give them handwritten cards with inspirational thoughts or words of advice.

Rosalie's kindness extended beyond children. She founded the Mason City chapter of the Humane Society, an action that Dixie Willson said stemmed from her mother's "deep and sincere concern for any suffering creature, especially for those who could not speak for themselves. No one else in town possessed the executive urge to devote the time, energy, thought and the necessary action to establish some sort of official protection for dumb animals, but several townspeople went along with her determination to do something about it," she said.

It was well known in Mason City that the horse trough installed downtown near the Congregational church was placed there at the behest of Rosalie Willson, and that the city council agreed to it partly out of need, but mostly just to get her off their back. Rosalie also lobbied city officials to appoint Rufus Nutting as the enforcement officer for the Humane Society, with authority to make arrests. She then worked with schools and churches to organize children as junior members of the Humane Society. She had 1,000 blue buttons made, with white stars on them, for the children to wear. Rosalie believed it was important for children to learn about kindness to animals because many of them had pets, all of them would one day grow up, and some would carry on the work of the Humane Society. Many of the youngsters who proudly wore the buttons of the Junior Humane Society were the same kids who had come to her home a few years earlier for those informal kindergarten classes.

Her sense of propriety and plain common sense extended to matters much simpler than organizing a Humane Society, and sometimes to things over which she had little or no control. She frequently complained about how addresses on letters were written exactly backwards. In other words, the name of the recipient was the least important thing to the postman. Rosalie thought addresses should start with the name of the country, followed by the state, city, street address—and then the person's name. She did not address her own mail that way, but believed it should be the standard. Had she lived long enough, she would have appreciated zip codes. Undoubtedly, she would have thought it made sense to list them first.

Another one of her causes was the renaming of two local waterways. According to Rosalie, two creeks that flowed through Mason City were actually offshoots of the Winnebago River, which also meandered its way through town. These waterways should be referred to as rivers rather than creeks, declared Rosalie. One of the pair, Willow Creek, ran under the Superior Street bridge about five doors south of the Willson home. The other, Lime Creek, wasn't anywhere near the Willson place but, according to Rosalie, deserved the dignity of being called a river. She tried to convince city officials by informing them that Mason City was settled by Indians at the confluence of two *rivers*, that the source of those rivers was the Winnebago, and that calling them "creeks" was simply inappropriate. Nearly 70 years after her death, as Mason City entered the 21st century, Willow Creek is still Willow Creek, and Lime Creek is still Lime Creek.

In the late 1920s, the town of Forest City, in nearby Winnebago County, changed the name of a little stream to the Winnebago River as part of the community's 75th anniversary celebration. Ironically, the festivities to recognize this change took place during a drought. The dry spell had lasted so long that not a drop of water flowed in the "river." It was christened with water drawn from a faucet. Twenty-six years after his mother's death, Meredith Willson paid tribute to her by making "River City" the setting of his most famous work, *The Music Man*.

Two things that were "Papa's doings" in the Willson household were making buckwheat cakes for the family for breakfast, and oyster stew for an evening meal. John Willson was a redhead who said he grew his whiskers only once—when he successfully fooled the Indiana jurists about his age when he was taking the bar exam. According to Dixie, both parents had a lot to do with the success enjoyed by their kids. "Our dad was a pretty fine fellow," she wrote years later, "rarely talented, devoted to his family and responsible in a great big way for whatever fine qualities any of his children possess." What Dixie did not say was that John and Rosalie were also polar opposites in personality and temperament, a fact that had a significant influence on the lives of their children.

Rosalie Willson was outwardly content with her life as a wife, mother, kindergarten teacher, Sunday School superintendent, and protector of children and animals. She almost never traveled. According to Meredith, with the exception of two trips to visit her sister in Topeka, Kansas, and a short journey to Charles City, 30 miles east of Mason City, to attend a funeral, Rosalie never left Mason City from the time she moved there until the day she died in 1931. Rosalie supervised the Sunday School for more than three decades; her husband rarely set foot inside a church. It was Rosalie, and not John, who said grace at the dinner table and special prayers at Thanksgiving and Christmas. While Rosalie spent a lot of time with her own and other people's children, her husband often remained aloof and removed from their activities. He was a loving father, but lived on a different familial plane. And yet, he had the ability to light up a child's face with a single comment. Meredith once said that one of his father's favorite expressions was to look at one of his son's playmates and say, "Why, you're gettin' tall enough to vote!"

One particularly vivid childhood memory of his father stuck with Meredith to the end of his life. One day, he and his Papa were walking home from a ball game at the local park. John was walking curbside, with Meredith on the inside. When his father spotted an empty liquor bottle up ahead on the ground in Meredith's path, he quickly sidestepped across so that he could stand between his son and the evil bottle.

John Willson loved to play cribbage, checkers, and to work puzzles—crossword puzzles, jigsaw puzzles, and anything that required mental dexterity. "I like to work out puzzles very well and can hardly lay one down until I have it solved," he once said. He also loved baseball and believed it was a game that could build a man's character. According to the *Mason City Globe-Gazette*, Meredith's father was the first man in Cerro Gordo County, Iowa, to throw a curve ball, a feat he accomplished on July 4, 1884—yet another first for a Willson.

He had learned how to throw a curve ball at Notre Dame, and had just returned after completing his first year. The locals urged him to join the town team in an Independence Day game against the Rockwell-Dougherty club, named for two neighboring towns known for raising strong farmers and good ballplayers. The *Globe-Gazette* reported that:

> The red-headed kid who was doing the pitching for Mason City, so proud of his curve, was ignominiously chased to centerfield several times by the irate batters. After being properly scared to death, John would throw a straight ball and Johnny Campbell, Jim Treaton, and Donny Conners, or one of the Kelsh boys, would hit one a mile over the teams and buggies out into the long grass and it was lost . . .
>
> So after a hectic two hours, Mason City was returned a winner by a score of 6 to 5. If association rules had adequate protection for the umpire and pitcher, the game would probably have resulted in a 6-0 shutout, as the curve ball, when it has never been seen by a batter before, is an unsolvable riddle.

John liked to tell the story of his first paying job—catching gophers for his father for two cents an animal. "But I never got paid," he said. "He told me I would have no use for it, and he gave me a note which I still have." It was an important early life lesson between Alonzo and his son, between two Willson men; one who knew the value of a dollar, and one who was learning about it.

Father Willson was also a talented musician. "He played a very good piano," remembered his daughter, "a beautiful guitar, and spent more time at home in family singing than we devoted to anything else as a group." He also liked to read and write poetry. "Is there anything finer than a phrase such as 'man's inhumanity to man makes countless thousands more,'" he once asked, quoting Robert Burns, his favorite poet. On Dixie's 31st birthday, her father wrote a poem and sent it to her:

> *I was just a young man,*
> *Very near twenty-four*
> *When I first saw my sweetheart*
> *With curls half a score*
> *She had no nice clothes on*
> *In fact, I declare*
> *She had less upon her*
> *Than Eve used to wear.*
> *But I didn't care*
> *A red cent for her clothes.*
> *What I liked about her*
> *Was her cute little nose*
>
> *And her shelly-like ears*
> *Oh so dainty and pink*
> *And her silky brown hair*
> *that was just bound to kink.*
> *And her dark, dreamy eyes*
> *With a baby-like stare*
> *That looked right a-past me*
> *'s if I wasn't there.*
> *She was little and sweet.*
> *Just the girlie for me*
> *And twas only with her*
> *That I wanted to be.*
> *It was long years ago*
> *When this passion I had*

But she's my sweetheart yet
Because I am her dad.

Music was a large part of the family life of John and Rosalie Willson and
their children. Dixie, Cedric and Meredith, being the offspring of the
Sunday School matron, were in most of the pageants and musicals put on
by the Congregational church. Rosalie Willson often laughed when people
asked her the secret to her success as a wife and mother. "Prayers and
banjos," she would answer. Music, believed Rosalie, was a window to the
soul, and poor music in a home was better than none at all.

Dixie, being 10 years older than Cedric and 12 years older than
Meredith, was out on her own much earlier than the other children and
headed for an illustrious career as an author, poet, and screenwriter. Had
Meredith Willson grown up to become a plumber, car salesman, or real
estate broker—or even an engineer like Cedric—the literary legend from
Mason City, Iowa, today would be Dixie Willson. And according to Dixie,
she owed it all to her father, mother—and a book.

"When our dad was 23 years old, and an amazingly serious boy whose
biggest drams even then were of a fine family of talented children," she
reminisced, "he came across a large imposing book which I hope is still in
the book case of my room at 314 So. Penn." The book—Dixie recalled the
title as *Prenatal Influence*—"outlined how potential parents could, from
the moment they knew they were to have a child, make and mold that
child's future into anything they wanted it to be."

When John and Rosalie discovered they were expecting, "they talked it
over and decided they would like to have an author for a child." Within a
short time, "fine engravings and copied photographs of great authors and
poets" were hung on the walls, and a "bust in bronze of a child reading a
book" was brought into the house. "Dad, who enjoyed reading aloud,"
Dixie remembered, "brought home everything he could find to read and
discuss concerning the lives of great writers and their work."

Dixie's earliest recollections were an urge to "write write write" in every
spare moment. "I was no more than ten when, instead of playing, I would
hurry home to a small desk Mama put in my room where, in my school
notebooks I would writes stories and plays while the neighborhood kids
romped outside."

John and Rosalie used the same "method" on their other children.
When Cedric was due, explained Dixie, "they decided on a business man

and bent all effort toward that." The same held true with her youngest brother. "When Meredith was due they discussed the future of this child and decided on a musician. All over our house pictures went up of great musicians. A bronze figure of Wagner . . .Books about music and composers and musicians were read aloud by Dad and re-read by Mother."

Dixie rapidly developed into a talented young writer (although hard work and firm discipline likely attributed more to the result than a few pictures on the wall and a nearby copy of *Prental Influence.*) In April of 1907, when she was 16 years old, she entered and won a writing contest intended for adults and sponsored by Munsing Underwear. The company was seeking testimonials for its products. Dixie's winning entry was a poem that began:

> *Say —I wonder if any of you kids*
> *Have got a dad like mine*
> *Who keeps a tellin' all the while*
> *Just how you ought to shine*
> *At home and school and everywhere*
> *Just 'cause you've got good underwear.*
> *Did you ever wear that Munsing stuff?*
> *It's mighty good and that's no bluff.*

Dixie's poem concluded with:

> And well, I guess that's all I'll say
> 'bout underwear, but anyway
> You just remember what he said
> When he was puttin' me to bed—
> Be thankful—always—everywhere
> That you have Munsing Underwear.

The Munsing company said it got entries from 5,000 adults and one child. Dixie won $25 but she also got the first taste of what she wanted to do for the rest of her life.

In February of 1914, Dixie wrote a three-act play called *The Blue Heron* that was produced by the Civic League in her hometown and presented at the local theater. Fueled by its success and with the encouragement of family and friends, she wrote another play. *The Paradise Man* was produced in November of 1914—just nine months after *The Blue Heron.*

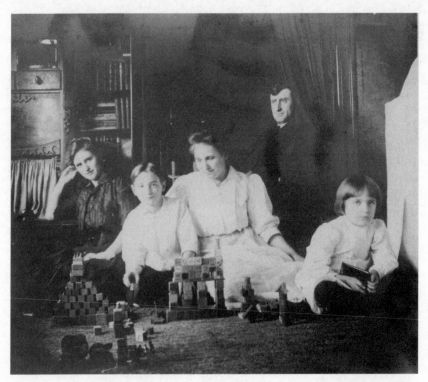

One of the few Willson family photos in existence of John, Rosalie, and all three children. From left to right: Dixie, Cedric, Rosalie, John, and Meredith, circa 1906. *MCPLA*

By this time, Dixie was 24 and about to break away from the family cocoon in Mason City. On October 19, 1915, she married Benjamin Lampert and the couple moved to Wisconsin. Before long, Dixie found herself in New York, pursuing her dream much like her youngest brother would do a few years later.

Meredith's earliest memory stretched back to the age of four, when he used to watch Charlie Rau, one of the church members, operate a contraption that projected images wherever the machine was pointed. Charlie painted the Star of Bethlehem on a slide and used it in the Christmas contata, pointing the machine toward the ceiling so the star hovered over the little children in the Christmas pageant of 1906. Charlie sometimes needed assistance sorting all of his slides during a program, and Cedric was enlisted to help him. Years later, Meredith recalled the pride he and his brother felt when Mr. Rau shouted, "Will Cedric Willson please come to the balcony!"

Meredith's stage debut in 1906 would eventually become one of the favorite Willson family stories. The setting was a Christmas pageant directed by his mother at the Congregational church. The precocious four-year-old took his place on the stage as one of the shepherds. A little girl who played Sara, the innkeeper's wife, announced that they would learn the significance of the night from Joseph. The performers and the audience were silent, awaiting Joseph's arrival on stage. After a few moments, young Meredith announced stoically, "the good father Joseph will be here in a minute. He has gone to the toilet."

Two years later Meredith was on stage at the Princess Theater in Mason City. He played a frog and jumped around stage in a green suit holding two wires in his mouth. When he bit the wires, the frog's eyes lit up, delighting the audience and earning Meredith his first pay for a performance—one penny.

In another play Meredith, at age seven, portrayed a boy lost in the woods with a little girl. With darkness setting in, the script called for him to provide some reassuring words to his female companion by telling her, "we

Rosalie Willson watches as her sons, Cedric (left) and Meredith (right), practice the piano. To the left of the piano is John Willson's guitar, which Dixie said he played quite well. Rosalie believed music was a window to the soul, and that poor music in a home was better than no music at all. *MCPLA*

will be safe, Francesca, if we sit beneath this sheltering greenwood tree 'til dawn." As he started to sit, Meredith discovered that his tight, velvet pants were beginning to rip at the seat. He eased up calmly and changed the script: "Francesca," he asked, "shall we stand beneath this greenwood tree 'til dawn?"

Before long, Meredith became less interested in acting and more interested in music. Dixie said that even as a young child, Meredith could make music on just about anything—on pieces of scrap pipe in the backyard, on his mother's sherbet glasses, and on the strings inside the big piano in the Willson home.

The boy who would grow up to provide music and joy to the world was a jovial youngster. According to those that remembered him, he had rosy cheeks, eyes that flashed with enthusiasm, and an infectious grin—all part of a personality energized with a spirit of trying to make sure everyone in his midst was having a good time. When the neighborhood children weren't involved in one of his mother's impromptu productions requiring youthful performances, they played marbles, Cowboys and Indians, and mumbletypeg, a game that involved throwing a knife from a variety of positions with the intention of sticking it firmly into the ground. Traditionally, the loser had to pull a wooden peg from the soil with his teeth.

Kids on the block like Marjorie Sale, who lived next door to the Willsons, and Art Swanson, who lived a half-block away in the big corner house on the northeast side of the street, loved to run around the neighborhood. Foot races up and down the street were a favorite pastime. Marjorie, a few years younger than Meredith, was the fastest runner of the bunch. Once, when she was far ahead of her playmates, she stopped to rest. As she lay on the grass eating an apple, Meredith came up to her, pointed a finger, and panted, "you will die if you eat an apple lying down." Then he laughed and continued running down the street.

Meredith, remembered Marjorie, was the neighborhood leader. Even at that age, he showed personality traits that would stay with him the rest of his life—the ability to step forward and lead when a leader was required, to create when creation was needed, and to get everyone involved when involvement was necessary. Often, when he and his friends were looking for something to do, it was Meredith who took over, initiating bird watching excursions, showing off the white mice he was raising, or teasing the girls.

Rosalie often laughed at her youngest son's antics and sometimes affectionately called him "Glory." The nickname prompted Cedric to look at his little brother and say, "Good morning, Glory!" a rare burst of humor for the oldest Willson son. While Meredith had the positive attitude and disposition of his mother, Cedric was quieter and, even as a youngster, almost businesslike in his approach to life's daily routine. In the summertime, the Willson brothers operated a lemonade stand on the curb in front of their home. While there is no written record of how the stand was run, it is well within reason to believe that Meredith solicited and entertained the customers while Cedric poured the lemonade and kept track of the pennies and nickels they took in.

Unlike many boys of his day and age, Meredith wasn't much of a baseball fan. In fact, he didn't even know one Major League team from another. About the only time he displayed interest in the sport was during the World Series, when the *Globe-Gazette* kept passers-by informed of the progress of the games by posting painted signs in the front window with the inning, score, and balls and strikes. Meredith didn't care who won or lost—especially since he often didn't even know who was playing—but he later recalled the "window World Series" gave him the same kind of butterflies in the stomach that he got when he was sitting in school, listening to circus parade music playing outside.

While many boys dreamed of growing up and someday playing in the World Series, Meredith dreamed of growing up and playing in an orchestra. He not only listened to the circus music—and most any other music within earshot—but enjoyed speaking with the performers who trouped through Mason City. Whenever he could, he would find his way backstage at a theater or go behind the big top at the circus so that he could listen to the entertainers and soak up the show biz atmosphere, musty as it was on the hot summer nights in Mason City.

Willson liked to recall things by the sounds they made. In his autobiography and in numerous radio interviews over the years, he recounted many of the sounds of his childhood. Two that he recalled distinctly were his mother playing "The Church in the Wildwoods" on the black upright piano in the parlor of the family home on Sunday morning—a prelude to the three trips to the church that day, and the sound of his first flute, the one delivered from the company in Chicago by his cousin Walter, who was the mailman.

But the piano came first. Rosalie began Meredith's music lessons at the age of six. Dixie clearly recalled "the endless hours" her mother spent around the upright teaching the youngster. The budding musician quickly outgrew Rosalie's talents and soon required a more experienced piano teacher. When he decided a few years later to take up the flute, Rosalie walked across Mason City in January "in the wind and snow to discuss borrowing the money for it from Ed Clark." Excitement rippled through the Willson home when the instrument finally arrived.

Although his piano instructor found a book on how to play the flute and tried to teach him, Meredith—who already had natural ability in music and an enormous eagerness to learn all he could—learned the most from Squiz Hazleton, a traveling musician who came through Mason City to play in the theater orchestra. Meredith studied for a year with Squiz. The relationship ended when, in a careless moment, Hazleton confided to John Willson, who was paying for the lessons, that Meredith knew more about playing the flute than Hazleton! After that, remembered Dixie, "Dad hunted all over the state to find a teacher for Meredith. He finally engaged one who had to make a weekly trip from Minneapolis for the lesson."

Two years later, Meredith, by then a high school freshman, was playing first flute in the Mason City High School band. He was also daydreaming about someday being known as: "Meredith Willson, first flute for John Philip Sousa, Sousa's Band." Many seeds of his future were planted and nurtured during Meredith's tenure with the school band. On November 24, 1916, the *Globe-Gazette* printed a story under the headline, "Boys Must Keep Out of Billiard Establishments." As is quite often the case at this time of year," admonished the paper, "when the evenings are the longest, it has become necessary for the proper authorities to take steps to curb the propensity of high school boys to play pool and billiards in the public pool halls, and of some of the proprietors—in violation of the law—to let them." There are, continued the article, "but few places, however, where boys known to be of tender years, are permitted to play pool, most of the places trying to obey the law strictly. School authorities made the rounds of the places this week and published a warning against letting the school boys use the tables."

Forty-one years later, Meredith Willson's *The Music Man* opened on Broadway. The story involved a con man trying to get the residents of River City to go along with his plan of selling musical instruments to youngsters to start a band—to keep them out of the pool halls.

By the time Meredith was at the age when boys frequented the pool hall, he, Cedric, and Harold Keidle, had formed a trio called "The Jones Brothers." Their favorite hang-out was Vance's Music Store in downtown Mason City. They rarely bought anything. Instead, the freeloaders listened to records and thumbed through sheet music, trying to memorize the notes so they wouldn't have to pay for it. John Vance ran the store. His mother, Jessie, had started the business in 1910. About a year later, her son began working there and eventually took over ownership. John Vance Jr. later succeeded his father as owner. Willson always remembered the store and those years fondly. Indeed, the hometown music store stayed with him as a beacon of his childhood, and he remained friends with the Vances for the rest of his life.

The summer after his freshman year of high school, Meredith landed his first paying job as a musician with an orchestra at Lake Okiboji, a resort town about 100 miles west of Mason City. In addition to his flute, Willson was expected to play the piccolo, which he was capable of doing. There was only one problem—he didn't own one. Before heading off to Okiboji he finally bought something at Vance's—a silver piccolo for $96, to be paid off at $12 a week for eight weeks. Since the Okiboji season was eight weeks long and Willson was paid $12 a week, his work for the entire summer went to pay off the piccolo.

The orchestra leader, Emery Moore, was called into the armed services and missed the last week of the concert season. Young Meredith was pressed into duty to fill in. After sitting down to play a while, he stood up to and directed the band. When the excited youngster took his seat again, he accidentally sat on his piccolo, bending it in the process. Thus the sum total of his first job as a professional musician was a break-even proposition: he worked eight weeks and had a bent piccolo to show for it.

Hazel Erwin Griffith, who was four years older than Meredith, played the piano in the orchestra that summer and later married one of the men who founded it. She said Meredith had not yet turned 16. In an interview at the time of the premiere of the film version of *The Music Man*, she recalled the night he sat on his piccolo. "I've never seen a man so sad. That piccolo stayed bent for years. He even played that same one when he took his first big job at the Winter Garden Theater in New York." Meredith was "a fine flute player," she explained, "but I confess I never really ever thought he would be a big-time success. I just thought he would end up as a musician."

According to Hazel, her father, J. H. Griffith, was Mason City's leading barber and John Willson was one of his best customers. In the film version of *The Music Man*, there are three scenes in which "Jim Griffith's Shave & Haircut Parlor" is prominently seen in the background. Hazel Griffith Erwin was forever grateful. "Through all of his success," she said of her boyhood friend, "Mere has not gone high hat."

Dixie had moved to New York in 1918 to try to make it as a writer. Once settled, she convinced her father to let Meredith, who was 16 at the time, come for a visit because she was certain that he would someday come to New York to carve out his career. John Willson agreed and sent his youngest son off on a train for the big city. On the night he arrived, Dixie took Meredith for a ride on a double-decker bus so that he could get a glimpse of the bright lights and glitz that she was sure would thrill him. She was wrong. As the bus rounded a corner near Times Square, Meredith spotted a large, electronic calendar-clock on one of New York's skyscrapers and took particular note of the date—July 12. "Look at that, sis," he said. "We're missing the county fair."

Peggy Wilson, Meredith's childhood sweetheart. In his high school year book, *The Masonian*, Meredith wrote his goal: "Consolidate the Wilsons." The couple married in 1920 without fanfare—or family. *MCPLA*

Meredith graduated from Mason City High School in 1919. His high school yearbook, *The Masonian,* yields many insights into the ambitious teenager's interests. He was in the high school band, orchestra, and glee club for all four years, and the chorus for three. He appeared in the school opera as a sophomore, and took part in the minstrel show during his senior year.

In the yearbook of 1919, students were allowed to include a favorite phrase or expression underneath the listing of their name and school activities. Many of the expressions show the maturity level of the students or their hopes or dreams or, in some cases, whatever happened to be on their mind at the moment. Classmate Lydia Crosby wrote, "she knows what she knows when she knows it." Helen Trissell's words of wisdom explained that "she needs no eulogy; she speaks for herself." Elsie Erickson wrote, "women are entitled to life, liberty, and the pursuit of man." Meredith Willson wrote simply, "great men are not always wise."

Perhaps more revealing is another yearbook inclusion, this one dealing with goals for the future. Willson's goal had nothing to do with flutes or piccolos or pioneers. He wrote as his goal: "Consolidate the Wilsons."

Meredith had been dating Elizabeth "Peggy" Wilson, the pretty daughter of the city engineer in Mason City. Within a year after his graduation from high school, Meredith Willson, who had already been to New York and back, and Peggy Wilson, his sweetheart, would be man and wife. And by marrying Peggy Wilson, Meredith accomplished one of his first goals in life: the Wil(l)sons were now "consolidated."

He was 18, less than a year younger than his bride.

The Mason City Municipal Band with its ambitious young flute player, Meredith Willson (second from left). Frank Simon, who played in the John Philip Sousa Band and was also a talent scout for Sousa, made a guest appearance in Mason City, heard Willson play, and encouraged Sousa to hire him. "The kid plays like an angel," reported Simon. Willson was hired without an audition. *MCPLA*

Chapter 2

"The Iowa Toscanini."

— Ben Gross, *New York Daily News*

Learning the Trade

Willson was an accomplished musician by the time he graduated from high school. By 1920, at the age of 18, he left the security of small town Iowa for New York because of the opportunities offered by the big city. One was the chance to study at the Damrosch Institute of Musical Art (now known as the Julliard School of Music). Another was the chance to fulfill an ambition he'd had since he first became serious about music: he wanted to play in John Philip Sousa's band.

"I was a gangly 18 when I began to feel my britches were getting too big for Mason City," he said in a 1949 radio interview. "So I decided to expand. New York was just about the right size." He took the train from Mason City to New York and got quite a send-off. "Of course, Mama and Papa were there, but I didn't expect the whole band." The "band" was Mason City High School's finest, dressed and drilled to give its most ambitious (and soon to be most celebrated) member a rousing send off. He left for New

York, Meredith later explained, with Papa's fried chicken, Mama's prayers, a mail-order flute, and a bent piccolo in his pocket.

Once in the metropolis, he studied flute with George Barrere, a world-famous flutist, different in about every way imaginable from Squiz Hazleton back in Mason City. In addition to being experienced and polished, Barrere also knew how a young musician could get a job in New York City. He introduced Willson to other flute players who had been his students, professionals like Lem Williams and Billy Kincaid. Their advice to the aspiring musician was that he should hang around the union hall and let it be known he was looking for work. And that is exactly what Willson did.

Before too long a man approached him and asked if he would substitute for him that night at the Winter Garden. The Winter Garden was one of New York's most prestigious theaters and Willson jumped at the chance. Excitedly, he telegraphed a message home to his parents, informing them of the Winter Garden gig. Following the man's directions, Meredith took the subway to Houston Street and then walked to his destination. To his utter dismay, it was not The Winter Garden Theater, but simply "The Winter Garden," a burlesque house rather incongruently tucked over a kosher market. Still, a job was a job. Willson finished and arrived home at 1:00 a.m. A telegram from his parents was stuck in his door: "always knew you'd make good." Another job came along quickly, this one at the more respectable Crescent Theater, where Meredith earned $52.50 a week, enough to enable him to pay for his flute lessons and also take some courses at the Damrosch Institute. Just six months later, at the age of 19, the Mason City native landed a job as a flute player—in the Sousa band.

John Philip Sousa is best remembered for his stirring, patriotic march, "The Stars and Stripes Forever." He was born in Washington D.C. in 1854 and, like his young protégé Willson, became interested in music at a very early age. Sousa published his first musical composition in 1872, and was the musical conductor for Gilbert & Sullivan's *H.M.S. Pinafore* on Broadway in 1875. He became the leader of the U.S. Marine Band in 1880, and in that capacity served under Presidents Rutherford B. Hayes, James A. Garfield, Chester Arthur, and Benjamin Harrison. He directed the Marine Band from 1880 to 1892 and toured the country with it. Shortly after the 1892 tour, David Blakely, a promoter, encouraged Sousa to start his own civilian concert band. "Sousa's New Marine Band" made its debut on September 26, 1892, in Plainfield, New Jersey. It became "The Sousa Band" after its leader received criticism from Washington politicians about using the Marine name in a civilian outfit. Sousa wrote "The Stars and Stripes

John Philip Sousa. The great bandmaster hired Willson without an audition. *MCPLA*

Forever" in 1896. His band toured Europe three times between 1900 and 1905, and went on a world tour in 1910. Sousa joined the Naval reserve in 1917 to help with the war effort, and then continued to tour with his band after the end of World War I. By this time he was one of the most famous band leaders in the world.

Frank Simon was a great cornet player in the Sousa band, the only band member hired without an audition. Sousa took him on the recommendation of a Cincinnati musician whose judgment he trusted. Simon and the Sousa band performed in Mason City in October of 1919 in a concert sponsored by the American Legion post. In 1920, Simon returned to Mason City as guest soloist with the city's municipal band. He was also on a talent search for Sousa's band. It was during this visit that he met Willson and heard him play. Simon wrote to Sousa and recommended to the old maestro that he hire the youngster to play in the band. Willson "plays like an angel!" wrote Simon. Sousa relied on Simon's advice, and

Willson became the second person to be hired by Sousa without a personal audition.

Willson toured the country with the band for three years. Sousa was old-fashioned and had strict standards he expected his band members to live up to. Band members were required to wear their uniforms at all times—white shirts with stiff collars and cuffs under a heavy uniform coat. That rule was relaxed only for mornings in the summertime. It was said that if you could make it through Sousa's rehearsals, you could make it anywhere. By the time Willson joined the band, Sousa had been at it for 50 years, and there wasn't much he hadn't encountered at one time or another. The demanding rigors of steady rehearsals and performances had begun to tire the old leader. As he got older, he slowly relaxed his strict conduct and dress code—for rehearsals, anyway. As a result, they weren't as exhausting for Willson as they had been for two previous generations of band members—but the expectations for excellence had not relaxed at all.

Every Sousa concert season ended with a grand performance at Madison Square Garden. It was a longstanding tradition that former Sousa band members would squeeze into their old uniforms and come to the concert dressed just as they had when they played for him. Most brought their instruments with them. The finale was unfailingly "The Stars and Stripes Forever," with the piccolo players, including Willson, marching down front to the footlights of the stage, just a few feet in front of the cheering audience. In Willson's first appearance at one of these season-ending concerts, there were 16 piccolos, 40 trumpets, 30 trombones and 22 drum players. Having experienced a musical extravaganza such as that, it would be little stretch of the imagination for a young musician 30 years later to envision seventy-six trombones leading a big parade.

Willson's air of confidence as a teenager performing for a man of Sousa's stature was a characteristic that served him well throughout his life. He was able to associate and mix and mingle confidently with people who had achieved greatness because he had the courage—the pioneer spirit his father had spoken of so often. This quality enabled him to play successfully for Sousa and then move on to perform for five years with Arturo Toscanini and the New York Philharmonic Orchestra; to work with scientist Lee deForest on his invention that eventually led to the use of sound with motion pictures; to work with Charlie Chaplin, the greatest comedian of the silent film era, and to write the music for his first "talkie" called *The Great Dictator*; to become one of the great stars of radio and one of the early musicians and performers on television; to write the words and music to *The Music Man*, one of the greatest musical hits of Broadway of all time; and to have one of his songs, "Till There Was You," recorded by the Beatles.

Willson displayed two other traits that also served him long and well. He wasn't shy about approaching strangers, and he wasn't afraid of being embarrassed. He believed it was natural for people to be scared when they met influential people, but it was important to act as if you were not at all nervous. To Willson, it was simply mind over matter. If you pretended you were not nervous in the presence of greatness, you would also act appropriately. In an orchestra, he said, the conductor is sometimes intimidated by the performers because they are the ones who know whether the conductor is competent or not—and the orchestra members are often intimidated by the conductor just because he's the conductor! It is interesting to note that Theodore Roosevelt, who was president when Willson was a boy, expressed exactly the same view about overcoming fright. In his autobiography, Roosevelt offered the example of a man being able to shoot bottles off a fence post. If the man ever encountered a bear at the same distance as the bottles on the fence post, he ought to be able to fearlessly shoot the bear. The key was to pretend there was no fear. It is not known whether Willson read Roosevelt's book and adopted his philosophy, but it is the type of book that John Willson would have had in his house.

Meredith once explained that he learned never to worry about embarrassing experiences because for every one that you're involved in, there's someone somewhere who has done something more embarrassing. The passing of years erased the embarrassment and turned it into an anecdote. He felt so confident about laughing off embarrassing moments that he entitled his second book *Eggs I Have Laid*. And he laid some classics. He once met a couple by the name of Mr. and Mrs. Bottom. Years later, he ran into them again and called them by name. Mrs. Bottom was impressed that he had remembered and asked him how he was able to remember things that well. "I always connect a name with a face," said Willson who was immediately horrified at the what he had just uttered. But in time, he said years later, it became nothing more than an amusing tale.

This was the philosophy of the young musician in New York who played for Sousa for three years and then joined the New York Philharmonic Orchestra where he played for Toscanini for almost six more. Toscanini was a contemporary of Sousa but he became famous in his native Italy before coming to the United States. He was the principal conductor of Italy's most renowned opera house, La Scala, from 1898 to 1908. After he reached America's shores, Toscanini became the conductor of the Metropolitan Opera Company in New York, a prestigious position

Arturo Toscanini. Willson later said the conductor could lead an orchestra with his eyes. *MCPLA*

he held for six years. He then spent many years with the New York Philharmonic Orchestra, where Willson crossed paths with him in 1924.

The year before he started playing for Toscanini, Willson had another encounter with greatness. In 1923, he got a chance to work with a genius in another field, Dr. Lee deForest. The inventor would one day utilize vacuum tubes to revolutionize motion pictures with sound, an achievement that would eventually make television a reality. In 1923, deForest was conducting sound experiments in his New York apartment. Willson, who was 21 at the time, was paid to go to his apartment every morning at 8:00 a.m. and play scales while deForest tried to record the sound on film.

When he would play it back, Willson's flute was almost impossible to hear because of all the static and background noise. Although Willson was at first disappointed, deForest explained that static and background noise meant that sound was indeed being transmitted. The young Willson marveled at deForest's patience, at how he would listen to scratchy noises every day and then rip apart the wiring in his studio every night and start all over again. DeForest had the same kind of mentality often attributed to Thomas Edison, the attitude of knowing that if you tried something 100 times and failed every time, that it had been a productive day because you had learned 100 ways that something didn't work.

The November 21, 1923, edition of the *Mason City Globe-Gazette* kept the home folks up to date on the latest developments of their native son:

The new success of the phono film on which Dr. Lee deForest, inventor of the audion tube, has been working during the past winter and which is now perfected, is due in part, according in a letter from deForest himself, to the assistance of Meredith Willson . . . who has been playing in the Rivoli and Rialto theaters in New York during the winter. The new process is one by which music or voice is recorded on a motion picture film and which is reproduced when the film is run off. Mr. Willson, who was a flute soloist in the band of John Philip Sousa for two years, assisted Dr. deForest by playing for him. Now that the experiments have been completed and the phono film is a practical reality, deForest expressed his deep appreciation of the former Mason City boy's help.

While deForest was a model of patience, Toscanini was a prime example of a person who could easily scare the trousers off a young musician. The Italian conductor was a perfectionist with a violent temper. It was rumored he could conduct an orchestra with his eyes, without ever moving his arms up and down. He later conducted the NBC Symphony Orchestra, which had been created especially for him. Toscanini, Willson once said, had an ear so amazing it could probably hear grass grow. And he also had an incredible memory. Toscanini memorized the pieces he conducted, which allowed him to keep his eyes on his orchestra—which is perhaps where the rumor about conducting with his eyes came from.

One day during rehearsal, Toscanini winced as a sour note coursed its way to his ears. He turned sharply to a clarinet player and said sternly, "F sharp! F sharp!" The rehearsal resumed and soon Toscanini stopped it yet again, repeating the same admonition to the same clarinet player: "F sharp! F sharp!" When the same thing happened a third time, someone hurried over to the clarinet player and pleaded with him to comply with the maestro's instructions. The unnerved musician assured him that he was playing an F sharp. As the musician talked, he raised his clarinet and blew a little bit of moisture that had collected under the keys, a common practice. An obviously frustrated Toscanini resumed the rehearsal, and the orchestra played. This time, however, the maestro smiled at the clarinet player as if to say, "Finally, an F sharp!" The musician had been playing the same note for the entire rehearsal. The moisture beneath the key had altered the sound so slightly that the man playing it couldn't hear the difference—but Toscanini could.

Thirty years later, Ben Gross, reporting in the *New York Daily News,* looked back on Meredith Willson's career and made a comparison that Willson himself would have considered of the highest order.

Willson, explained Gross, was "the Iowa Toscanini."

The Willson children, Cedric (left), Dixie (center), and Meredith (right), fulfilled their parents' expectations of them by becoming, respectively, a businessman, author, and musician. *MCPLA*

Chapter 3

"My brother is a very smart man in the industrial field. In fact,
he is an expert. I don't mind telling that to you but
it's the first time I've ever told it to him."

— *Meredith Willson, in the* New York Herald Tribune

The "Other" Willsons

The Willsons were one of Mason City's most distinguished and successful families. As America rolled into the 1920s, the three Willson children were on the brink of launching extraordinary careers. Meredith was in New York and about to hook up with the Sousa band. Dixie, who by that time was 29, had established herself as a writer and was already in New York, which must have provided some comfort for her ambitious younger brother. Cedric was about to join Meredith in the Sousa band before attending college with intentions of becoming an engineer.

Dixie, the first of the trio to marry, tied the knot with Ben Harrison Lampert in Mason City on October 19, 1915. Outwardly, at least, she married well. Lampert worked for the county engineer in Cerro Gordo County, of which Mason City was the county seat. He was also the son of a

Rosalie and her children pose for a photographer. Cedric is on the left and Meredith is on the right. Dixie stands behind them. MCPLA

prominent Wisconsin businessman. When Lampert's father was elected to the United States Congress, the couple moved to Oshkosh, Wisconsin, so that Ben could manage his father's business affairs. Unfortunately, the fabric of the union began fraying rather quickly. Dixie, who harbored aspirations of becoming a famous writer, could not handle the role of the doting housewife.

Dixie Willson rides a circus elephant, part of the on-the-job training she gave herself in preparation for writing a book about circus life. *MCPLA*

She and Lampert divorced amicably about a year after their marriage and Dixie headed for Chicago, where she landed a job as a dancer in a theater production. Her big break arrived when the show transferred to New York, where Dixie got a job in vaudeville and soon thereafter, as a chorus girl for the Ziegfeld Follies. She had the same ability as her youngest brother to make good contacts.

In 1920, after working for two years as a critic with the Fox Film Company, Dixie quit and joined the Ringling Brothers Circus because she wanted to write a book about circus life from an insider's point of view. Her book, *Where The World Folds Up at Night*, was her first real success as an author. It was about this time that she also became an accomplished writer of short stories. One of her stories, "God Gave Me 20 Cents," was made into a motion picture that was shown at the opening of the Paramount Theater

Dixie in a director's chair in Hollywood. In 1924, she won an award comparable to today's Academy Award for one of her screenplays. *MCPLA*

in New York. Her screenplay for the movie won an award comparable to today's Academy Awards.

With a film credit firmly affixed to her blossoming resume, Dixie journeyed to Hollywood in 1928 to continue writing screenplays. The *New York Times* reported that her annual income was $50,000—a grand sum at that time—and that her screenplays were selling for $10,000. The prolific Willson daughter also continued writing books and short stories. In 1937, she hit upon the idea of creating a "theater kit" for children. The kit contained a script, props, and costumes for children to put on their own theater productions—just as Dixie, Cedric, and Meredith had done under their mother's direction when they were growing up. Although Dixie created more than a dozen different show boxes, slow sales put an end to the creative idea. In 1938, Dixie worked with Betty Crocker at General Mills and had some of her recipes published in the famed Betty Crocker cookbooks.

As her career blossomed, Dixie reconfirmed her pledge to remain single, saying that for her, a husband was excess baggage. She kept that pledge until November 26, 1945, when she married Charles Hayden, manager of a repertory theater company in New York that was doing one of her plays. An example of Dixie's impulsive nature was found on the guest list at her wedding—a daughter named Dana. Fourteen years earlier, Dixie had shown up in Mason City from California with the infant. At the time, Dixie explained that the baby was the illegitimate child of a Hollywood starlet and that she had taken up the responsibility for raising her.

Dixie also wrote poetry, a talent she said she inherited from her father. One verse she penned for Volland, a marketer of birthday cards, was one of the company's best sellers:

> Count your gardens by the flowers,
> Never by the leaves that fall.
> Count your days by golden hours,
> Don't remember clouds at all.
> Count your nights by stars, not shadows
> Count your life by hopes, not fears
> And dear one, on this, your birthday,
> Count your age by friends, not years.

Although like her father in many ways, she also carried the independent spirit and feisty attitude that her mother often displayed—and she sometimes surprised her mother with it. Two days before Christmas in 1930, she was walking in downtown Mason City with her mother when a thief grabbed her purse and ran down an alley. To the utter astonishment of the elder Willson, her 40-year-old daughter chased the culprit and caught him. Then she proceeded to bargain with him, offering to split whatever cash was in the purse if he would give the handbag back to her. At first the thief balked, but Dixie's persuasion soon won him over. The only cash in the purse was a five dollar bill and three singles. The thief insisted on taking the five, saying he would buy "a good feed" with it. As he started to depart, he asked if his victim intended to follow him. She promised she wouldn't, after which the thief shook hands with her, wished her a Merry Christmas and ran off. Dixie had her purse, and the man was $5.00 richer.

Unbeknownst to the thief, the purse had a concealed inner lining with $500.00 in cash and a certified check for $333.00. The story of how Dixie bargained with a thief, "split" the money with him, and then shook hands on the deal, made good reading in the next day's newspapers. "Now here I have gone all over the world, been with all types of people and have been to all kinds of places and yet I had to come to my own hometown to be robbed," she said.

Like Meredith, Dixie's younger brother Cedric was a good musician who had toured with the Sousa band as a bassoonist. The boys differed in their aspirations, however, for Cedric had no intention of making a career in music. At the behest of his mother, Cedric had learned to play a second instrument, in addition to the piano, so that he would stand out from the other children. Cedric chose the bassoon, or as he called it later in his life, "the squawking hat rack." When the Sousa band broke up, he decided to go back to school instead of continuing on as a musician, a decision he never regretted. "It was the smartest thing I ever did," he said in a 1966 interview with the *Dallas Morning News.* "They were calling me a chump at the time, choosing college and turning down a theater orchestra job. But I could see myself, at 70, bent at the shoulders and always with white hair, climbing out of an orchestra pit."

Cedric had the gift of music that the rest of the family had, but in personality, he was businesslike, much like his father. Whereas Dixie and Meredith were outgoing and extremely talkative, Cedric was reserved and not given to idle banter. He graduated from the University of Kansas in 1925 with a degree in civil engineering, performed graduate work at both Kansas and New York University, and earned a master's degree in civil engineering. He worked for Texas Industries Inc. for 25 years, rising to the level of vice president and was considered one of the nation's experts in the field of lightweight aggregate and concrete products. His career did not bring him the fame heaped upon his older sister and younger brother, but it did earn him national acclaim among his peers for his expertise in his chosen field.

Cedric's brother and sister were sensitive to the fact that their professions provided them with more publicity than Cedric received. In 1957, on the eve of the Broadway opening of *The Music Man*, Meredith praised Cedric in an interview with the *New York Herald Tribune*, saying, "My brother is a very smart man in the industrial field. Light aggregate concrete. In fact, he is an expert. I don't mind telling that to you but it's the first time I've ever told it to him."

When the hometown *Globe-Gazette* was preparing an article on Cedric, the paper contacted Dixie for some background information. She dispatched the needed information promptly and then penned another note the following day to W. Earl Hall, the paper's editor. "I thought I'd add this postscript since I do so want this story of Ced's new plant to be just right," she explained. "In my letter about it, sent you yesterday, I spoke of the fact that both Meredith and I have frequently been in the news whereas Ced seldom is. Of course, I shouldn't want any reference to this fact in the story; I want this story to be all Ced's excepting for the mere mention that we are his brother and sister."

The Willsons were a storybook family—an entrepreneurial father who was an excellent provider and who inspired his children to be the best that they could be; a kind, energetic mother who was the spiritual leader of the family; and three children who were about to experience phenomenal success in their lives.

Meredith had been courting Peggy Wilson, his high school sweetheart who had stayed home and attended college when Meredith left for New York to launch his career in 1919. Many in Mason City probably envisioned a lavish wedding for the pair, given the prominence of their respective families. Instead, the 18-year-old Meredith returned from the big city less than a year after he left and swept Peggy off to Albert Lea, Minnesota, about 30 miles north of Mason City, where he married her on August 29, 1920. Neither family was told of the secret union.

The couple intended to pursue their individual paths, with Meredith returning to New York and Peggy returning to college to complete her teaching degree. But the young lovers decided they could not bear to be apart. Ten minutes before Willson's train was scheduled to leave for New York, they broke the news of their marriage to their families and made arrangements to travel to New York together to begin their new life. Exactly why Meredith and Peggy decided to eschew the expected local fanfare and elope without informing family and friends is not known. Meredith never spoke or wrote publicly about the matter.

But all was not well in River City. Beneath the pleasant facade presented by the Willson family swirled troubled waters that had a profound impact on Meredith's life. Indeed, on all of the children. Little is known about the extent and depth of the problems that existed between John and Rosalie. All indications are that they were severe, longstanding—and intensely bitter. On Christmas Day 1919, for example, Rosalie placed an armful of presents before John on the dinner table. An argument ensued and he swept them from the table and refused to speak to her. That incident, as well as the letter printed below, are part of the public record in Cerro Gordo County District Court.

On January 11, 1920, almost certainly after the couple had separated, John wrote this scathing letter to his wife of 31 years:

Rose:

For the past twenty-five [sic] years, it has been plain to me, and probably to you, that we are a mismated couple. Our view of life is so diametrically opposite [sic] that no harmony has been, or can be possible, except by keeping away from one another. In view of the fact that we have three children, whose future has been a claim upon us, I have stayed with you and done the best I could to help rear them to manhood and womanhood.

This being now accomplished, there is nothing now to hold us together except the bonds of a sinful union. I regret that the children have had to listen too [sic] disagreeable and inharmonious conversations, and have naturally acquired a querulous demeanor that will handicap them in life. I hope and believe tho [sic] that they have, in the same time, acquired some practical common sense; otherwise our sacrifice will have been worse than in vain.

In the past, you have accused me openly and insinuated that I was every thing mean and crooked. You have misjudged and twisted in crime every act of mine; therein I sought my own kind of companionship. You have never liked the same kind of people or entertainment that I enjoy. Your attitude has been one of bigotry [sic] and a determined obstinacy [sic] to make me go your way or destroy me. The children have been put up to doing things contrary to my desires. You have searched my pockets, stolen, destroyed or

John Willson divorced his wife and married a woman four years younger than his daughter. *MCPLA*

concealed property, some of it belonging to neither you or me. You have at all times refused to go with me to live any place except your own choice.

You have always refused to sign any papers, thereby humiliating me before businessmen and injuring my standing and business ability and credit. I don't [sic] know whether it was jealousy that caused your action or not, but this kind of treatment has caused me to despise you and your ideas. You have always ignored my desire for personal contact and companionship, and your every word and act grates on my nerves until they have become raw and unstrung and are a menace to my health and usefulness [sic] in life. Life to me in your company has become simply a hell and not to be endured. I have become cross and boorish, and try as I may, I cannot be myself. I have not heart to work as my mind is in a constant turmoil.

If I force myself, when alone, into a tranquil [sic] state of mind, one insulting word or insinuation or some inane remark from you will make me ugly and miserable. No one else in the world affects me this way. To me you are inane and ignorant. You embody all that I despise. You are a good woman according to your lights, and if you lived in this world, instead of on some visionary and impractical plane, it would not be so impossible.

As you are, you are to me as a red rag is to a bull, and it is nothing short of a crime for me to continue to ruin your life and for you to ruin mine as we have been doing for the past years. Better a thousand times that we go our separate ways, as you have told me so often to do, in the past when I could not leave the children, and give each other a chance to get out of the remaining years of life whatever happiness we can.

"Rose" Willson in later life. After the bitter divorce, she always referred to herself as a widow. *MCPLA*

You are hampered by me in a thousand ways. If I were out of your way, you would be free to pursue your own ideas of life, and would no doubt feel a great burden lifted from your mind, even tho [sic] the (indistinct) notions, at the first glance. A quiet analysis of the situation, will, undoubtedly, tend to confirm you in the same conclusion to which I came long ago, that we will only have a fair chance to enjoy life when we are apart.

If we take the other horn of the dilemma, and you insist on keeping me to the marriage vow, I would, if I remained in your company, continue to grow more disagreeable than I have been, unsatisfied with life, unhappy, unsociable, as far as you are concerned, because as I see the helplessness of the struggle, I naturally see less to live for, and at the end I would probably choose to go out of my life before my natural time, seeking oblivion rather than hell on earth. It certainly would be no comfort to you knowing how I feel.

I ask you therefore to let us separate as all decent and well meaning persons ought to do who find that they are absolutely unsuited for each other. Let us at least be kind to each other and sensible in this.

In my opinion, there is but one life to live and that is the one here on earth. I am entitled to my opinion as much as you to yours. Thinking as I do, I believe I am entitled to get at least something out of this life, if possible. I have an honest effort to so change my nature as to comply with the environment that I have found myself (indistinct) by our union, and I have found that it cannot be done. To try is simply to destroy all that is good in me and all that is good in you. The greatest crime that can be committed by two people is to ruin their own lives and all those who come in contact with them by forcing themselves to live together when every instinct of their better natures tells them that they should be apart. I further believe it is the worst kind of adultery to cohabit with a person whom you dislike and with whom you have no friendly feeling even tho [sic] married to that person.

Your life has been so far, a failure to you. I know you so admit and I agree with you. Mine has been the same. Due to our marriage and living together. Both will continue to be so unless we do what we should do, get away from each other and give each the chance to repair the damage that has done so far as possible in the years remaining.

There is nothing to be gained by the continuation of the farce. In fact, I have made up my mind that I will not continue thus. If I did, I would grow crazy and I don't believe I am required to go that far. I should in time come to hate you so that I do not know what I might not do.

When you came to me, you had nothing of this worlds [sic] goods. I do not propose to leave you in this condition. I propose to endow you with $25,000 worth of property, which will yield you a good substantial living, and a chance to sell and reinvest in some other [sic] place or with a good prospect of advance here. As far as the children are concerned, they will be assisted by me to the limit of my ability as in the past. Their status will in no wise be changed. We cannot live their lives, we can only guide them, and we will be far better able to do so if we are apart than in the turmoil of a disrupted home.

You will be able to pursue the course you see fit without the hampering of my ideas. Your property will be unencumbered and you will have the chance to show how much better you can do with the pay envelope than I can. You will have a $25,000 start which I did not have, and no mill stone around your mental apparatus, which I have always had.

We owe, that I know of (I don't [sic] know your debts) about $25,000 and I will take over that burden, leaving you clear.

My expenses in taxes, interest and paying this $25,000 debt will take about all of the income of the property I keep, the same as it always has, but I can earn my living, I think, and give you yours, when I get free of the strain of the past years.

If you will agree to it, I will go to some distant point in Iowa, there take up my residence, and procure a divorce quietly by default and without any publicity or annoyance to you, deeding you the property proposed beforehand. If you will not agree, then I will go somewhere and try to get it anyway, because I think that when we separate, for the rest of our lives we should not be subjected to embarrassment as to our future movements. There can be no restitution to happiness and contentment if a shadow still hangs over us.

I will go away to live and you can do as seems best to you. Please consider this kindly, in the Christian spirit that you so conscientiously profess, and with the full knowledge that it is the only possible way to treat each other fairly and right. There can be no compromise, as I have reached the end as far as this way of living is concerned.

There has got to be a change, an end of this, and the time has come to be sensible. It is my [intent] to get this matter settled at once, so that I may seek some business which will be satisfactory and remunerative so that I may be able to help Ced thro [sic] his education and Meredith if he shall need my help. I am not young and the days of labor for me are short and the time is right for new fields. I wish to get at it now.

There is nothing to wait for except to get at a fair division of property and get what we have into such shape that it will not be endangered by extraneous circumstances. I do not wish to have more than I can give you. The only way I can engender a kindly feeling for you is for you to show me this once that you wish to have some respect for my feelings in this matter. You are set and stubborn, bigoted [sic], vain and have an insatiable desire to ape after people who are in better circumstances than we. You travel alone in your chosen sphere and I wish to get out of the way so that you may follow those inclinations unhindered. You will not go my way, you sneer at my friends and associates and I want to get you out of my way so that I can, without fear of insinuation or insult, associate with the class of people that I find to be the most honest and kind hearted and less hypocritical than the ones to whom you wish to attach me and yourself.

You have never given an inch. In your heart you still believe your ways are superior. You are a "Reiniger." I am not and cannot become one. When I think of the times you have humiliated me before businessmen, even until your grown children have been ashamed of your actions & begged for me, I grow to hate. It makes me rage inwardly now to think of the times without number that you have told me to pack up and go.

I don't think it best to tell the children, as it would simply upset their work and their minds and do no good. We are farther apart than Lucille and Ben ever were and even you would say they are better as they are. I will get a petition on the Jan. or Feb. term of some court and we will get it over and start on a new life unhindered by the divorce because I take it that you would not do so on account of what people will say. If you will, I am more than willing. I will only include such matters in my petition as will be sufficient and it will never be read by anyone but yourself who can and will act as your attorney to see that your property is secure.

Please do this for me and yourself and let me go away thinking of you kindly at last.

The divorce was an ugly and rather public affair. John even openly accused Rosalie of "spending Ced's college money on lawyers." After weeks of charges and countercharges, John and Rosalie Willson formally ended their union on February 5, 1920. "Rose" was granted the divorce on grounds of "cruel and inhuman treatment."

It did not take John long to find a new wife. The same year he was divorced, he married Minnie H. Hartzfeldt, a woman four years younger than his daughter Dixie. Instead of moving across the state and starting a new life, as he claimed he would in his caustic letter to Rosalie, John and his new bride took up residence at 313 S. Delaware Avenue—one block west of and behind the Willson family residence at 314 S. Pennsylvania (Superior) Avenue. Rosalie could look out her back window and see the home of her ex-husband and his new wife. She planted shrubs tall enough to block the distasteful view. From the time of her divorce until her death on September 15, 1931, Rosalie referred to herself as a widow.

John Willson died on January 10, 1931. It was shortly after her father's death that Dixie arrived in Mason City with baby Dana. In another display of rather bizarre behavior, Dixie convinced Minnie Hartzfeldt Willson, John's second wife and Dixie's stepmother who was four years younger than she, to keep Dana and raise her. After Minnie Willson died on December 2, 1940, the child resumed living with Dixie.

There is no definitive record as to how John's and Rosalie's divorce affected their grown children. In later years, Dixie spoke in loving terms about them and there is evidence that she kept up correspondence with both parents. There is also firm evidence that Cedric visited his mother whenever he returned to Mason City, but his relationship with his father after the divorce is unclear.

It is probable that the divorce in February soured any plans Meredith and Peggy might have harbored for a big wedding in Mason City—especially that year. The embarrassment of the split, coupled with its obvious deep-seated bitterness, may well have led to their quick and simple marriage in August. In all of the books, radio, and television broadcasts in which he referred to his family for the rest of his life, Meredith rarely mentioned his father beyond simple recollections of his childhood.

Once, when he was honored for his work with the Big Brother organization in Los Angeles, an agency that helps boys whose fathers have died, Willson confided to a *Los Angeles Times* reporter that his interest in the organization might stem from the fact that he didn't have as close a relationship with his father as he would have liked. The interviewer remembered that Willson mentioned it twice, at different times during the interview, but never elaborated beyond those few words.

In a 1970 interview with the *Washington Star*, Willson opened up about his youth and relationship with his father in far different terms than he ever had in the past. Up until that time, he had sung loving praises of his "Mama" and "Papa," and his books are full of stories of his comfortable and carefree life on Superior Avenue in Mason City. The *Washington Star* story, however, paints a sad portrait of a family life riven with parental divisiveness and a boy caught in the middle, utterly neglected by his father. "My mother and father already had a son and daughter, Cedric and Dixie. They were the apples of my father's eye. He was angry when my mother told him I was on the way. From that time on, my father never spoke directly to my mother by name and never in my lifetime did I hear my name pass through my father's lips."

Meredith never stopped yearning for his father's approbation and love. The elder Willson, explained his son, went to the Mayo Clinic in Rochester, Minnesota, for treatment of an ailment at a time when Meredith was playing with the Sousa band in a neighboring town. "I stopped in to see him and told him I was first flute with the Sousa band and playing a solo each day and maybe he'd like to hear me." Meredith then painted a sad portrait of his relationship with his dad. "I stood in that hospital room and played for him and he still wouldn't admit he appreciated it or I was talented or I was good or anything. I really think I sped his demise. That was the last time I saw him alive."

By that account, Willson did not see his father for the last seven years of John Willson's life. Every time Meredith and Peggy journeyed home to Mason City, the *Globe-Gazette* unfailingly noted the homecoming by saying they were visiting their mothers. (Peggy's father, Fred Wilson, had died on November 23, 1922, but Meredith's father lived for eleven years after divorcing Rosalie.)

In his three autobiographical books, *And There I Stood With My Piccolo*, *Eggs I Have Laid*, and *You Gotta Know The Territory*, Meredith never mentions his parents' divorce.

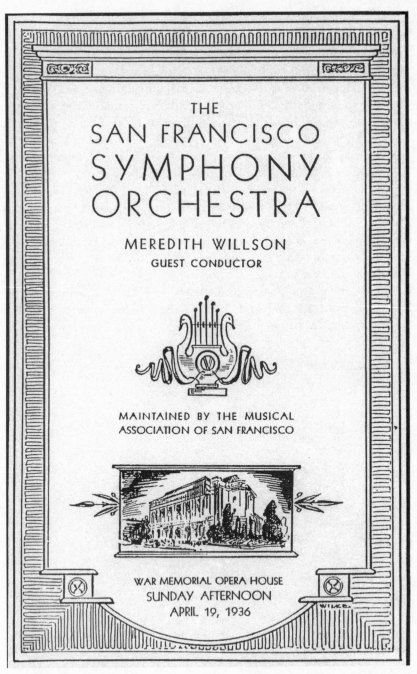

THE
SAN FRANCISCO
SYMPHONY
ORCHESTRA

MEREDITH WILLSON
GUEST CONDUCTOR

MAINTAINED BY THE MUSICAL
ASSOCIATION OF SAN FRANCISCO

WAR MEMORIAL OPERA HOUSE
SUNDAY AFTERNOON
APRIL 19, 1936

Program cover from the day Meredith Willson conducted his own symphony.
MCPLA

Chapter 4

"Their happy and devoted married life has
played no small part in Meredith's success."
— *Golden State Eggs Advertisement*

Doing a Greeley

eredith Willson liked to poke fun at himself. He not only
did it as part of his everyday conversation, but he even
wrote a book, *Eggs I Have Laid*, devoted entirely to that
very subject. His first book, *And There I Stood With My Piccolo*, took its
title from a story about an unnamed Maravian piccolo player who was in an
orchestra hired by a king to play during his supper. The orchestra played
well and the king was so impressed he told its members that they could all
go into the room where he kept his treasure and fill up their instruments
with gold pieces. "And there I stood with my piccolo," said the sheepish
musician.

Willson trouped for three years with the Sousa band, traveling all over
the country in his Brooks Brothers band uniform, playing in big cities like
New York and San Francisco, with appearances in Canada and Cuba as
well. Then it was on to the New York Philharmonic, where he not only
polished his skills as a musician, but rubbed elbows with some of the
world's greatest conductors. In time, he developed the urge to become a

conductor in his own right. He got a chance to do that very thing in June 1929 when the American Broadcasting Company (ABC) opened a new studio in Seattle, Washington. ABC sponsored the 70-piece American Philharmonic Orchestra, conducted by Francesco Longo, as well as several guest conductors. Some of the visiting conductors included Henry Hadley, Alfred Hertz, Karl Krueger, Michael Plastro—and R. Meredith Willson. The concerts were performed on Wednesday and Sunday afternoons in the football stadium at the University of Washington.

When Sousa, the wise old maestro and Willson mentor, learned of his protégé's opportunity, he expressed his best wishes for the ambitious young musician but imparted a shrewd piece of advice. Good luck, he said—but keep your instruments handy. "I can't honestly say I took Seattle by storm, but I can say that Seattle took me by storm," joked Willson many years later. He arrived in the midst of one of Seattle's frequent rainy seasons, and the outdoor concerts were a bust. He described his first attempt at being a conductor by saying, "I laid a very large egg in the shadow of Mount Ranier."

Willson returned to New York, as he described it, "a little short in the pocket." He quickly found work as a substitute piccolo player in a band that played in Central Park. One night, as he was walking to the performance, he ran into Sousa on the streets of New York. Mindful of Sousa's advice to him, and reluctant to tell him how he had flopped in Seattle, Willson lied to his old conductor by telling him he was leading the orchestra in Central Park. Willson should have known better. He knew the concert that night would end with a stirring rendition of Sousa's "The Stars and Stripes Forever"—that included the piccolo players marching down to the footlights as they played, the same routine Sousa's band had enacted when Willson played with it. On this particular night, Willson later recalled, as he blew into his instrument and scanned the audience, his gaze fell upon Sousa sitting in the front row. Their eyes met—"and there I stood with my piccolo," said Willson.

It is an amusing story and one in which Willson used himself as the hapless victim of ill-timed circumstance. It also demonstrates another classic Willson trait—embellishing the truth for the sake of good story. The events probably all occurred, but not in the sequence in which he described them. For example, Willson did not leave the Sousa band for the conductor's job in Seattle. In fact, he played with the New York Philharmonic Orchestra for five years after leaving Sousa's orchestra. Any break from playing with Sousa to try to make it in Seattle would have occurred between 1921 and 1923, the years he played with Sousa. But the job as orchestra leader in Seattle did not come up until 1929. It is conceivable that before he left for Seattle in 1929, he touched base with the old man who had given him his first big break, and that Sousa had provided him with the sound advice to "keep your instruments handy." But the only way the rest of the story could have occurred was for Willson to have returned to New York, a city teeming with seven million people, and to somehow have run into Sousa on the street.

Before he and wife Peggy ventured out to Seattle, Willson worked for NBC radio. It was in 1926, when the National Broadcasting System was being formed. He was still with the New York Philharmonic Orchestra, but moonlighting on the flute with an orchestra playing concert music in a little studio on the edge of Broadway. Little did he know then that the medium of radio would one day catapult him into national stardom. He received $14.00 for each performance, including rehearsal time and the hour-long broadcast.

That little moonlighting job afforded him the opportunity to be part of another first, to once again be a pioneer like his father and grandfather before him. NBC radio went on the air at 8:00 p.m. on November 15, 1926, and stayed on the air until 12:25 a.m. the next morning. It was heard on 25 stations, 21 of them charter affiliates. The other four were independent stations. The broadcast originated from the Waldorf-Astoria Hotel, one of New York's finest, and included appearances by famed humorist Will Rogers, the New York Symphony Orchestra, Albert Stoessel of the New York Oratorical Society, and several other bands and orchestras.

In addition to technicians, the NBC staff that night consisted of two men: Phillips Carlin and Graham McNamee. The latter was on the verge of a prominent sports broadcasting career during which he would inform the nation of some of the greatest sporting events of the early 20th century, including the 1927 boxing match between Jack Dempsey and Gene Tunney, remembered most for the famous "long count" that allowed Dempsey to get up off the canvas and eventually win the fight; and the 1932 World Series between the New York Yankees and Chicago Cubs in which Babe Ruth reportedly pointed to the outfield bleachers and called his shot before hitting a home run in the second game. McNamee is in the American Sportscasters Hall of Fame. Carlin became one of the great early announcers for NBC for shows such as the Palmolive Hour, Goodrich Hour, and Atwater Kent Hour, all named for their sponsors. He was one of the people responsible for the creation of the famous "NBC chimes," which became one of the identifying symbols of the network but were created as a signal to affiliates across the country that it was time for a station break. But on the night of November. 15, 1926, McNamee and Carlin were nothing more than "gophers" for the head liners.

Meredith and Peggy Willson's arrival in Seattle on June 4, 1929, was treated as a major event, and the pair were even greeted at the train station by Mayor Frank Edwards. Willson, only 27 years old, was touted as being the youngest philharmonic concertmaster in the country and he had high hopes for beginning a successful career as a conductor. But then it rained, and then it rained some more, and the disappointed but always hopeful Willson sought refuge in the comfort of a Seattle radio station—working indoors. He kicked off his new career at KJR radio as a flute player, and later became the station's musical director under a plan in which station ownership hoped to build a network starting on the west coast much like the National Broadcasting Company had done on the east coast. But the idea flopped, the network folded, and Willson and his wife headed back for New York. (If Willson ran into Sousa again after returning from Seattle, it was probably at this time.) Willson had developed good contacts on the west coast, and it wasn't long before he was working there again. In 1929, he wrote the musical scores for two movies, *Peacock Alley* and the *Lost Zeppelin*, two movie "talkies" that he had helped lay the groundwork for eight years earlier when he played the scales for deForest in the scientist's studio in New York. Meredith's next stop was San Francisco, where in 1930 he became musical director of KFRC Radio, a prominent station that often featured live performances by such stars of the era as Nelson Eddy, Kay Kyser, and Phil Harris.

The period of 1927 to 1937 has been described as the golden decade of radio in San Francisco. Both NBC and CBS, fledgling networks at that time, set up broadcast centers in San Francisco in an attempt to establish a west coast presence. When NBC went on the air on November 15, 1926, only two-thirds of its NBC title was true. It was indeed a broadcasting company, but it was "national" only in terms of the goals and dreams of its founders. In reality, its service stretched only as far as Denver because telephone lines for broadcasting had not been installed beyond the Rocky Mountains. The quickest solution was to, in effect, establish a second NBC network, originating from the west coast and heading east, toward the Rocky Mountains. The Pacific Coast Network, dubbed the Orange Network because of the color of its cable lines, was launched on April 5, 1927, from the Colonial Ballroom of the St. Francis Hotel in San Francisco. After a few speeches by NBC board members, the rest of the first broadcast was mainly music provided by the San Francisco Symphony Orchestra under the direction of Alfred Hertz.

When Willson and his wife arrived in San Francisco, they found themselves in the right place at the right time. Not only was the medium of radio about to take off, but so was the career of the young musician. Many programs that originated from San Francisco gained national prominence over the next several years. The most famous and most popular was "One Man's Family," which told the story, week after week, of family life in America as seen through the experiences of one particular fictional household. It was a novel concept at the time of its debut in 1932, but it was the beginning of what became a staple of radio broadcasting and, years later, television—the serial, the continuing saga of a family that captivated the imaginations of listeners and viewers all over the country. Willson would one day be a part of this genre on the Burns & Allen radio program, named after its stars, George Burns and Gracie Allen.

But in the early 1930s, he was busy on several other fronts. Willson was the musical director of "Carefree Carnival," a program of western music and skits, and before long assumed the reins as west coast musical director for NBC. It was an exciting time in the infancy of radio, and every day was a new adventure and experience. Often, only a few performers made up the entire cast of characters on programs such as "One Man's Family," because listeners only heard the voices. Thus it was cheaper to have each actor or actress portray two or three different parts. There were no lines to memorize. They all huddled around microphones and read from scripts with a sound effects man stationed nearby to provide rain hitting a roof, a knock on a door, or whatever noise the script demanded. Even though the performers, including Willson and his musicians, were heard and not seen, they all dressed formally—in case a sponsor showed up at the studio. Many of the shows carried the sponsors' names, such as the Palmolive Hour, sponsored by Palmolive soap, the Colgate Comedy Hour, sponsored by Colgate toothpaste, and the Texaco show, sponsored by the oil company of the same name. The sponsors paid the bills, and it was important that they be impressed with every aspect of the show, down to the attire worn behind the microphone.

While Willson made inroads in radio, he also took quite a liking to his new home. San Francisco and its citizens responded in kind. Herb Caen, columnist for the *San Francisco Chronicle*, wrote about Willson's Midwestern roots and his years with Sousa and the New York Philharmonic. But then, wrote Caen, "Willson did a Greeley" and wound up on the NBC staff in the Golden Gate city. The columnist was referring to Horace Greeley, a 19th century newspaperman whose advice to a young Easterner was to "go west, young man, and grow up with the country." Caen, who penned his own way to fame in the newspaper world, spent an afternoon with Willson and came away impressed. "It's a treat, indeed, to watch Willson in action. He's the symphony conductor, Hollywood style, come to life. He brings at least a dozen batons to the studio for each broadcast, and their mortality rate is high, so high, in fact that he keeps a stock of 25 extras always on hand. "His dark hair, usually neatly parted," continued Caen's descriptive pen, "becomes a waving mass as he leans from the podium and implores his musicians to 'Give! Give!' Each wave of his baton, each gesture with his left hand means something as he seeks to draw the utmost from the orchestra. And if he doesn't like someone's performance, he isn't hesitant in expressing his views." According to Caen,

> Musicians like Willson. We mean all types of musicians, from the most finished symphony soloist to the hottest 'jam' trumpeter. And where music is concerned, Willson is broad-minded. He thoroughly enjoyed New York's swing concert and he raves no end over performers like Benny Goodman, Tommy and Jimmy Dorsey, Red Norvo and Winny Mannone. But no matter what style Meredith Willson is called on to direct, he insists upon accuracy, brilliance, finish. Perfection is not enough. He seeks something even higher. And someday he'll find it.

It was during his time in San Francisco that Willson created a new show called "The Big Ten," in which he took the weekly list of the 10 most popular songs from *Variety* and had his orchestra play them on the air. An advertising agent from New York heard the show while he was in San Francisco on a business trip. He went back to the east coast and convinced officials at Lucky Strike cigarettes, one of his clients, to sponsor a show like that nationally. Lucky Strike quickly agreed and so did NBC, and the "Lucky Strike Hit Parade" was launched. According to Willson, he never got any money or credit for the idea. The name of the program was later changed to "Your Hit Parade," and had a long run on both radio and television.

Sometimes, Willson looked out the window of the 22nd floor of the NBC studios in San Francisco and daydreamed, just like he had as a child, peering out his bedroom window on Superior Avenue in Mason City. As he looked down from his office at NBC, he watched day by day as workers pieced together a magnificent structure that would be known to the world as the Golden Gate Bridge. It was these sights and sounds of San Francisco that inspired him to achieve yet another first in his life. On April 19, 1936, at the age of 33, Willson became the youngest conductor of the San Francisco Symphony Orchestra. He was the guest conductor at the War Memorial Opera House for a Sunday afternoon performance in which one of the symphonies was his own work entitled "Symphony in F Minor-a Symphony of San Francisco."

And San Francisco loved the attention. "Spirit of Great City Caught by Willson," heralded the headline in the *San Francisco Chronicle* over an article describing Willson as "handsome and charming and enormously gifted." In an editorial on Friday, April 17, two days before the concert, the newspaper urged its readers to attend in respect and recognition for the honor Willson had bestowed upon "his city"—a phrase that would have made residents of Mason City cringe.

Reviews of the symphony were generally favorable, and Willson was invited to perform it in other concerts throughout the country. One reviewer, however, damned Willson's creation with faint praise. According to Alfred Frankenstein, the music moved, was strong and colorful, and the instrumentation was "cleanly handled." But he was less charitable with Willson's attempt to connect it with San Francisco. "And now that the ice is broken, Willson would do well to dispense with the subtitle 'Symphony of San Francisco' and the rather obvious program associated with it," admonished the reviewer. "The program does not coincide with the music any too clearly, which is all to the good. Such 'explanations' of abstract music may have the virtue T.S. Eliot ascribes to literal meaning in poetry. They may serve like the bit of meat the burglar brings along to occupy the attention of the watchdog. But if the dog is of any value as a guardian, he will not be taken in twice by the same ruse."

After the concerts in San Francisco, Meredith and Peggy took a six-week vacation that included a cruise along the Panama Canal and two weeks of sightseeing and visiting old friends in New York. On the way back home, they stopped in Mason City to visit Peggy's mother and, as was always the case when the famed musician returned home, Meredith chatted with the local press.

In an interview with the *Globe-Gazette*, he quickly dispelled any notion that San Francisco had become his hometown. "Who knows? I might write a Mason City symphony," he said. "Mason City has plenty to crow about. I like it every time I come here."

Willson wrote a second symphony, "Symphony No. 2 in E Minor: The Missions of California," in 1940, but the composition did not receive the fanfare garnered by his inaugural work. Nearly six decades later the two symphonies were performed by the Moscow Symphony Orchestra, in Moscow, Russia. The 1998 performance was led by Los Angeles conductor William Stromberg. A music researcher in California had come across the symphonies and told Stromberg about them. The symphony orchestra in Russia was contracted because orchestra members overseas work cheaper than those in America. Recordings of the Willson symphonies were made, and are today available for sale on compact disks. The *Globe-Gazette*, which had closely tracked Willson's career throughout his adult life, arranged to have three music experts critique the symphonies more than a half century after they were written, and 15 years after Willson's death.

For conductor William Stromberg, the symphonies were "much more Gershwinesque than I would have imagined."

Steve Metcalf, a music critic for the *Hartford Courant*, reviewed the symphonies for his newspaper after coming across the compact disks and listening to them. "If they don't immediately seem like major discoveries," he wrote, "they are certainly important additions to the legacy of a true music man. They are nice pieces but it would be overstating it to say they are orchestral masterpieces."

Gilbert G. Lettow, the band director at Mason City High School where Willson played first flute 70 years earlier, said he liked some movements of the symphonies better than others. "What sticks out in my mind is that Meredith Willson was a brilliant, well-rounded musician. In assessing the symphonies, I think it's important to see them as another facet of an amazing talent."

Willson experienced a good run in San Francisco and seemingly could have spent the rest of his life there. As musical director of NBC for the West Coast, he was one of the most respected, and best known, musicians in the country. He had led the orchestra for three programs broadcast coast to coast—*Carefree Carnival, Saturday Nights*, and *The Wandering Minstrel*—composed and conducted two symphonies, and had become one of the youngest symphony conductors in the country. But the entertainment emphasis on the west coast, and in the country, was shifting to Los Angeles and Hollywood, in southern California, and Willson willingly and enthusiastically pulled up roots and followed it. NBC's blockbuster hit show, *Maxwell House Showboat*, which had been on the air since 1932 and had originated from New York City, was switching locales and moving to Los Angeles, but its musical director was not going with it. Willson was hired to replace him.

While Willson was fast becoming the most well-known musical director in the country, Peggy Willson was earning a reputation as a supportive wife and one half of one of tinsel town's most successful marriages. Her family and the Willsons had known each other for many years because the two mothers had been good friends and were pregnant at about the same time,

Mrs. Wilson with Peggy, who was born first, and Rosalie Willson with Meredith, who was born a few months later. Meredith and Peggy were childhood playmates and joked when Meredith was 9 and Peggy 10 about getting engaged.

Their love for each other had blossomed while both were students at Mason City High School. Peggy was just enough older than Meredith to be a year ahead of him in school, where she participated in the German Club and was one of the leads in the annual Thanksgiving play. The play was called "Rosalie"—just like the name of her boyfriend's mother, but this Rosalie was a maid, and Peggy Wilson had the title role. Also that year, she was a primary grade Sunday School teacher at the Congregational church, where her future mother-in-law was the superintendent.

When Willson graduated from high school in 1919, he went to New York to try to carve his niche as a musician, leaving Peggy behind to continue her education in Iowa. As related earlier, less than a year later he returned to Mason City and the two eloped. The newlyweds set up housekeeping at 100 Northern Avenue, Apartment 64, New York City. The landlord was the Rev. Don Bean, a pastor of a Congregational church in New York City, which probably pleased Rosalie Willson immensely back home in Iowa. While Meredith studied at the Damrosch Institute and played any musical job he could get at night, Peggy graduated from the Ethical Culture School in New York City, qualifying her to teach anywhere in New York state.

The new Mrs. Willson was photographed frequently with her famous husband, but little was written about her other than that she was a good wife. A 1926 *New York Times* newspaper article gave the impression from its headline that the story focused on Peggy and her happy marriage. "That Letter 'l' Only Rift in This Romance," said the headline, followed by a subhead that read "Mrs. Willson, Nee Wilson Has Difficult Time Signing Her Name"—a cute reference to the fact that Peggy Wilson had to add an 'l' to her last name when she married Meredith Willson. The story joked that the Willsons came within one `l' of having the perfect marriage, and that Peggy had to concentrate on spelling her new last name correctly after she was first married. The piece recounted the couple's romance, how they married quickly and came back to New York. The rest of the story was entirely about Willson and his career.

Peggy appeared in a 1930 full-page magazine advertisement for Golden State Eggs, the sponsor of Meredith's Monday night radio program on KFRC radio. In addition to promoting the eggs, Peggy shared with readers that her husband did not salt them, but did salt his grapefruit. Then the ad mentioned Peggy's contribution to the Willson's happy marriage in language and attitude typical of that era. "Their happy and devoted married life has played no small part in Meredith's success," it read. "This success has in part been due to Peggy's comprehension of and sympathetic interest in his problems."

In August of 1940, the *San Francisco Chronicle* reported on the Willsons' upcoming 20th wedding anniversary:

> Many stories have been written about ideal marriages, but none fits the plot better than the union of Peggy and Meredith Willson. This setting is the city where admittedly they spent the happiest years of their married life. Mr. and Mrs. Willson will celebrate their 20th anniversary amid a series of fetes to be tendered by their San Francisco friends. The Willsons are scheduled to arrive in San Francisco this morning for Willson's All-American concert at Treasure Island Tuesday night, when the noted young composer-conductor introduces to the Bay City his 'Missions of California' composition, Symphony No. 2 in E Minor.
>
> While Willson devotes his time to musical work, Mrs. Willson will make arrangements for the anniversary celebration on Thursday evening, August 29. Because it was in San Francisco that Willson first rose to fame, they consider it fitting that such an important day in their lives be spent here.

Peggy was often depicted in print as if her only role in life was as the wife of Meredith Willson. She enjoyed her time in California immensely, years that stood out in sharp contrast to the couple's meager beginnings in Apartment 64 in New York City two decades earlier. The Willson home in Los Angeles, "The House That Music Built," as one magazine referred to it, boasted a huge and ornately decorated living room, complete with a giant oval multi-colored braided rug that covered most of the polished hardwood floor beneath it. The dining room table and chairs were English prototype, adding to the colonial look and motif of the room. The master bedroom had a headboard made from two French provincial settees. Most of the rooms contained musical mementos, including Meredith's collection of miniature orchestras and orchestra leaders. One tiny band was made up of china cats. Another in the collection was made up entirely of flute players. The walls of the Willson den were decorated with plates adorned with the portraits of Liszt, Chopin, Grieg, Schubert, Beethoven, and Mendelssohn. Beneath each portrait were inscriptions of the first few bars of the most famous compositions of each composer.

The July 1945 issue of *American Home Magazine*, which sold on the news stand for 15 cents, couldn't resist mentioning Meredith's roots or his on-the-air antics, even in a story about the beautiful home he and Peggy had in California. "Every Thursday night, Meredith Willson, one of America's finest composers, walks up to an NBC microphone and gets into a discussion with George Burns and Gracie Allen. He gets great fun out of convincing listeners he is a dope—and yet he can conduct a great symphony orchestra through compositions by Bach or Beethoven." Willson, the article continued, "has finally achieved that 'home of their own' that he and his wife have dreamed of for years. It's a friendly place and furnished with old treasures picked up around the country—and fine old pieces brought from Iowa."

The Willsons did not have children—Meredith often said that his songs were his children—but there was usually a pet in the Willson home. For many years Emily, a black cat with a white mane, enjoyed the run of the house, much like a spoiled child. She knew how to get on the good side of her master. Often, when Meredith went to the piano and started playing, Emily jumped on top of it and watch him attentively.

Peggy Willson led a life of quiet elegance, and her marriage was the envy of many who were not as successful or content.

Meredith and Peggy strike a serious pose for a photographer during a visit to Mason City in 1936. *MCPLA*

Chapter 5

"Meredith Willson is a symbol of the new Hollywood."
— Tom Moriarty

What Every Young
Musician Should Know

*I*n 1938, the Willsons moved to southern California, where Meredith took over as musical director for some of NBC's most successful programs. His resume by this time was impressive. He had played in the Sousa band and the New York Philharmonic Orchestra under Toscanini, performed experiments with Dr. deForest, and worked as a conductor and at a radio station in Seattle. In addition, he had performed for his own radio shows in San Francisco and served as musical director of the western division of the National Broadcasting Company.

Willson also had 19 published compositions for orchestra to his credit, including the "Symphony No. 1 in F Minor–A Symphony of San Francisco," which was first performed under his direction on April 19, 1936; "Radio City Suite," first performed by Dr. Frank Black with the NBC Symphony in 1935; "Song of Steel," first performed under the direction of John Charles

Thomas in 1934; and "Parade Fantastique," performed by the New York Philharmonic in 1930.

As musically talented as he was, one of his most endearing qualities was his sense of humor and ability to laugh at himself. Both of these traits were liberally sprinkled throughout a manuscript Willson wrote that was published by the Robbins Music Corporation under the title *What Every Young Musician Should Know.* In its Foreword, Willson apologizes for even attempting to write the booklet, which totaled 40 pages, because of all the other writings available on the same subject. But, he explained, sometimes the youthful American mind has absorbing solutions to practical problems that differ from the standard music textbooks.

Any doubt that Willson's work would be different than the standard textbook is quickly alleviated in the preface: "The purpose of this preface is to enable me to state clearly my loathing for a certain device that frequently clutters up many otherwise lucid books about music. I refer to that rude, impudent, interrupting, irritating, thought breaker-upper known as the footnote." At the end of this paragraph Willson inserted an asterisk (*), one of the standard indications of a footnote. At the bottom of the page, readers found the following: "This is the first and last footnote you will encounter in this book."

"As a matter of fact," the preface continued, "I have the sneaking suspicion that nobody reads prefaces anyhow, so I will throw you a curve and discuss my preface under the heading of (turn the page) Chapter One."

And thus began Willson's dissertation on the finer points of music. "A blood curdling scream escaped the white lips of voluptuous young Amanda Whittlebottom. Before the scream dies away, I will hurry into my reasons for writing this book and what I hope to accomplish thereby." Willson discussed his goal for penning the book in the first place—to provide practical information on studio and dance band orchestration. *What Every Young Musician Should Know* included chapters on meeting the orchestra, how to hold a baton, hand signals, how to get blood out of a turnip, and musical jargon. The latter included entries like these:

"Rip"—several anticipated grace notes from the brass section;
"Sock"—exaggerating the rhythm tempo;
"Bend"—saxophones, brass and strings smearing a sustained note;
"Button"—the final chord;
"Spat"—the shortest possible cymbal crash;
"Jig" or "Bounce"—a tempo indication usually concerning tunes of
   a dotted eighth and sixteenth nature;
"Lick"—referring to any ad lib solo passage;

"Riff"—exactly the same thing as a lick;

"Slurp"—the tying of two or more notes together by means of a glissando;

Willson unabashedly demonstrated his musical preferences when he included "swing" in his list of jargon. "I'll frankly confess," he wrote," I cannot give you any coherent definition."

Four full pages of specific directions on how to wield a baton were included, including the caution about one thing readers would discover: they are not leading the orchestra; it's the other way around. The most important thing about the "technique of the stick," as Willson called it, was that it must never be stationary. Once the music starts, the stick must move constantly. Willson also described various hand signals and explained why they were necessary. He harkened back to the early days of NBC, when Graham McNamee and Phillips Carlin had been promoted from their opening night floor sweeping duties but often found themselves as the only staff in the studio. When one of them was on the air, the other was scurrying around, setting up the studio for the next show, arranging microphones and making sure performers for that show and the next show were lined up and ready to go. Because most studios operated like this, hand signals were developed to give directions without speaking, so as not to disturb what was being broadcast over the airwaves.

Some of those signals included:

The Mussolini salute, showing the flat of the hand: When the orchestra saw the flat of the hand, that was the signal to play the show's theme song;

One finger raised in the air: This told the orchestra to take the first ending and repeat the strain they were playing. Two fingers indicated to do the same with the second ending;

Closed fist: With this signal, the orchestra was to conclude whatever it was playing, at the end of the phrase.

Finger drawn across the throat: This meant "cut"—stop the music.

Palms moving toward each other: This signaled that the performer needed to move closer to the microphone. Conversely, palms moving away from one another was the signal that the performer was too close and needed to back away.

These two ads appeared in the back of Willson's book, *What Every Young Musician Should Know.* MCPLA

"And so in this year of 1938, if you are extemporaneously conducting an orchestra anywhere on the globe, the chances are that the orchestra musicians would immediately respond to the signals," Willson informed his readers.

Willson's booklet sold for $1.00, and included advertisements on its back pages for three other Robbins books: Frank Skinner's *New Method of Orchestra Scoring*, $2.00; Spud Murphy's *Swing Arranging Method*, $1.00; and *Arranging for Modern Dance and Orchestra*, by Arthur Lange, which had a more hefty $5.00 price tag.

What Every Musician Should Know was not a literary success, but it did represent another first for Willson—a published, albeit thin book—and it embodied not only his courage to venture into new territory, but also his humor, his knowledge and his ability to teach, three that by now were well-established ingredients in his formula for success.

The same year the book was published, a writer named Tom Moriarty described Willson as "a symbol of the new Hollywood," and, watching him conduct one night, offered his readers a vivid description of the man with a stick in his hand. He was, Moriarty wrote, "a tall and dark young chap madly cutting the air with a baton in high right hand and holding his left hand rigidly on high as if balancing a street car strap. All the men and women operating that mass of violins and trumpets and cellos paid eager mind to the baleful glaze in the eyes of the young man with the black hair whipping around his forehead." Moriarty was amazed at what Willson had accomplished at such a young age. He pointed out that an actor can become a star when a good screen test lands him a major motion picture role, and that an athlete can do the same with a good game or tournament. But Moriarty said that in music, it takes the "puttering patience" of a great mathematician, the strength and fortitude of a housewife with two young children and no one at home to help, and the idealism of a social worker. And in addition to all of that, said Moriarty, it takes talent.

The writer fretted and cautioned Willson about some of his radio broadcasts in which he was the musical conductor for a program as well as the announcer and therefore often the stooge, the butt of some of the jokes that went out over the air. Moriarty pointed to what he considered Willson's important works—his symphonies and his book *What Every Young Musician Should Know*—as the road on which he should continue traveling. "Hokey comedy parts on the radio are OK, I guess, and make the orchestra leader who can handle them twice as valuable to the sponsor, wrote Moriarty, "but the hell of it is that they are not exactly in the idiom of Symphony No. 1 in F-Minor."

But hokey comedy was what was paying the bills on radio in those days. An orchestra leader, in order to make good, had to do more than wave a baton. He also had to be a combination of a straight man for all the comics, an actor with lines to read, and master of ceremonies, to keep the shows moving along. All of this was in addition to leading the orchestra. "I can remember, in those dear dead days beyond recall, when an orchestra leader was just that and everybody was satisfied with his lot," Willson said in 1938. "Between numbers, he just sat around and watched everyone else at work. But all of this has changed now . . . The average baton waver now may be called upon to do anything from a dramatic sketch to serving as a foil for a comedian's jokes. In his spare time, he leads the orchestra. Sometimes he even delegates that job to one of his stooges while he's busy stooging for the star of the show. "This, of course, is all to the leader's advantage when you consider it makes him a more valuable addition to any program, helps him develop any hidden talents he may have and tabs him a more interesting personality in the eyes of the listener."

Willson's course required him to perform a delicate balancing act in each of the worlds to which Moriarty alluded—the composing of serious music that would maintain his position as one of the nation's leading conductors and song writers, and the ability to engage in comedic banter that would keep a nation of listeners tuning in week after week. Both skills thrilled sponsors, and in broadcasting, that was the name of the game.

A new and rather bold show called *The Maxwell House Showboat* debuted in 1932. The musical-variety program offered entertainment that was supposed to make the listeners believe they were enjoying live performances while lazily cruising on a paddle boat. As a result, it was critical to the show's success that the hour-long presentation offer not only good entertainment, but attract an imaginative audience. It got both, and soon became the number one show on radio. In 1937, NBC decided to move the program from New York to Los Angeles, and Meredith Willson was tapped as its new musical director.

Willson didn't think it mattered much whether the show originated from New York or California because both were far removed from the Mississippi River, which the "paddle boat" was supposedly navigating. Every week, the show opened with the sound of a paddle boat swishing along, a calliope piping in the background. Before long, Willson's orchestra would play and a chorus would sing "here comes the showboat, here comes the showboat." It was a great opening because it easily identified the show and created a sense of anticipation for the listeners across the nation, sitting in front of their radios waiting to be entertained.

And they were entertained—although sometimes not exactly as the sponsors hoped. The opening night of the show in California went smoothly except for one thing: the studio clock was 90 seconds slow, a lifetime in live radio. Unfortunately, no one noticed it except a couple of crew members who couldn't get anybody's attention. When the west coast version of "The Maxwell House Showboat" went on the air that night, instead of the swishing of a paddle wheel amid orchestra music and singing, millions of Americans heard encouraging small-talk such as "give 'em hell, Hattie" and "this is it, kid." The rest of the show went along without a hitch, red faces notwithstanding.

A year later, NBC launched a new variety show called *Good News*. It was perhaps the first "spin-off" because it featured as its guests many of the performers from *Showboat*, a program it helped to promote. Before long *Good News* had a unique identity all of its own, partly because of Willson, who had moved over to that show to lead the music. One of the reasons NBC moved its variety shows to the west coast was to take advantage of the huge reservoir of Hollywood stars who lived and worked in the Los Angeles basin. Most of them jumped at the chance to appear on the radio shows, perform for the listening audience, joke with the hosts, and plug their latest movies.

Film star Robert Young, who later in his career would endear himself to television audiences as the wholesome dad on *Father Knows Best* and the wise doctor on *Marcus Welby, M. D.,* was the host of *Good News.* Fannie Brice and Frank Morgan were two of the show's regulars. Brice was a comedienne with a background in burlesque, vaudeville, film, and the Ziegfeld Follies. In 1936, she created a radio character called Baby Snooks, which made frequent appearances until her death in 1951. *Funny Girl,* the movie starring Barbra Streisand, is based on Brice's life. Frank Morgan had a long career in films but is best known for his portrayal of the tin man in the film classic *The Wizard of Oz.*

Among the stars of the day who participated with Brice and Morgan, and with Willson nearby leading the orchestra, were Jeanette MacDonald, Allan Jones, Sophie Tucker, Eleanor Powell, Joan Crawford, Robert Taylor, Clark Gable, Spencer Tracy, and Judy Garland. Thousands of Americans tuned in every Thursday night to hear the bawdy Brice and Morgan exchange quips, to find out who was going to be on the show that night, and to hear Willson's music.

Like *Showboat* a year earlier, *Good News* also had a surprise in its debut. The guest lineup for the first show was magnificent—Jeanette MacDonald, Alan Jones, Judy Garland, Sophie Tucker and others. Featured dancers were Eleanor Powell and George Murphy, an actor who one day would be elected United States senator from California. The climax of the show was to have been a tap dance by a lanky, light-footed young man by the name of Buddy Ebsen. Ebsen would go on to make quite a name for himself on three television shows in as many decades, first as Davey Crockett's friend on Disney's *Davey Crockett* TV series, as the rustic and reckless father Jed Clampett on *The Beverly Hillbillies,* and as Barnaby Jones, the rumpled but wise private detective on the show with the same name.

All the young Ebsen was expected to do on the debut of *Good News* was to come out and do his tap dancing routine, a feat he could do so well that listeners could close their eyes, hear the tap-tap-tap, and feel like they were right on the edge of the dance floor watching him. But one thing went wrong: Ebsen forgot to wear his tap shoes! The listeners were treated to what Willson recalled was about 16 measures of silence while Ebsen pranced through his routine on sponge-soled footwear.

The guest list for the final show of the 1939 season, broadcast June 29, 1939, included most of the cast of the soon-to-be-released movie *The Wizard of Oz*, produced by Metro Goldwyn Mayer, which also provided the studio for the *Good News* program. That broadcast aptly demonstrated the range of what Willson was expected to do in terms of both music and comedy. In the first part of the show, his orchestra played a medley of songs from the movie. It was the first time the "Wizard of Oz Overture" had been performed live. The show concluded with a stirring rendition of "Over the Rainbow," and when it was over, host Robert Young complimented Willson on the beauty of the presentation. "Shucks, Bob, twern't nothing," drawled Willson. "*The Wizard of Oz* is my favorite story. I remember the first time it was ever read to me. I was sitting in my teacher's lap. I was 18 then."

By this time Willson had mastered the art of walking the tightrope between the rambling, stammering fool as the foil for many of the show's jokes, and the serious musician providing beautiful music for America. Sometimes, the two images collided. On one occasion, Dr. Albert Coates, a distinguished British conductor who was now directing the Los Angeles Philharmonic, came to the NBC studio to watch Willson conduct the orchestra during the *Good News* program. He was mortified as he watched Willson engage in what he considered stupid jokes and mindless prattle with Morgan, the co-host. Coates simply got up and walked out.

Whether Willson chased him down and apologized or Coates simply disappeared into the night depends on which version of the story you believe, because the tale was told and retold many times by those who witnessed it. One thing for certain is that the Willson "schtick" was not something the stuffy but brilliant British conductor was accustomed to seeing.

Coates was born in St. Petersburg, Russia, to British parents and studied music both in Russia and England. He was a large man who sweated profusely when conducting his orchestras. One of his early mentors told him he was more suited to direct an orchestra with a whip rather than a baton. Despite his often caustic behavior, he was held in high regard in both Russia and England. The British entrusted him with the duty of conducting the orchestra at many important functions. The Russians appointed him chief conductor of the Imperial Opera. One reviewer observed that "he could conduct the British works with proper reserve and yet lead the Russian ones with unbuttoned abandon and yet was able to gain respect for both which testifies to his truly cosmopolitan credentials."

It would seem that the humorless conductor was versatile enough to handle everything from classical music to opera—but was unable to appreciate the versatility of the young American conductor who could switch from music to comedy at the flash of a cue card.

It was an example of what Willson had been warned about years before—the mixing of mindless comedy with musical integrity. But Willson had not only learned how to do it, he was a master at it. Sponsors loved it, the public adored it, and Willson was making a good living at it. The Coates reaction was a tiny little ripple in a very large pond.

Willson, meanwhile, was succeeding at both forms of entertainment. He wrote a song entitled "You and I" that was intended to be the theme song for *Good News*. It wound up, however, being the number one song in the country for nine months, earning it a place on the Lucky Strike *Hit Parade* program, the offshoot of the Willson idea for which he received no money or recognition. One of the unique qualities of "You and I" was that the entire lyric was one single, non-stop unbroken sentence.

In 1941, Meredith stopped by the KGLO radio studio in Mason City to plug his song, "You and I," which was the number one hit in the country. Willson confessed later that the photo was staged; he wasn't singing and the microphone wasn't on. *MCPLA*

Willson journeyed home to Mason City in August of 1941. There, he posed for a photograph holding the sheet music to "You and I" and singing into a microphone, or so it appeared. The microphone was not even turned on, and Willson wasn't really singing because, as he explained, "I sing best silently." When asked about it, he had difficulty explaining his most recent success, the tremendous popularity of the *Good News* theme song. "It took me 30 years to find the qualities necessary for one," he said, referring to writing a hit song, "and how I wish I had a recipe to write one every week. "'You and I' had a natural simplicity and personal quality in its lyrics. In a 'boy and girl' song, this is absolutely necessary. I just happened to hit upon the lucky combination of a simple melody with lyrics that fit it ideally."

In another interview, Willson talked about what it took to write a song. "When it comes to music, I am one of those people who lives strictly in the present," he explained. "Nothing is more important to me than the composition or orchestration I am working on at the moment. It is always my masterpiece and I never fail to wonder why my past work cannot measure up to the present. I may have just completed an original manuscript that was four or five weeks in the writing," he continued, "then turn around and work out a novelty arrangement of 'Dipsy Doodle' for Fanny Brice. So long as I am working on 'Dipsy Doodle,' I am absolutely convinced it excels anything I have ever done."

Willson's next song, "Two in Love," a sequel to his smash hit "You and I," was a success but did not have the sustained popularity of the theme song. Peggy Willson, in a rare conversation with a newspaper reporter, said she liked it better than "You and I."

In 1941, with the *Good News* theme song still at the top of the charts, *Super Song Book* magazine credited Willson with creating more musical firsts and creative programming than anyone else on the air. It cited:

* *Chiffon Jazz*, a 1929 Willson innovation, the first program to use violins and woodwinds for popular dance music instead of brasses and saxophones;

* His 1932 program, *Waltz Time*, a half-hour program devoted entirely to waltzes, which was common in the 1940s but had never been done until Willson tried it;

* *Concert in Rhythm*, another 1932 program, this one aimed at making popular dance music something that could be enjoyed by people who choose only to listen to it;

* The 1934 *Big Ten* program, forerunner to the Lucky Strike Hit Parade;

* A 1940 program in which ten top songwriters were commissioned to do short pieces in a classic form, the first time anything like that had ever been done on radio. The composers and what they came up with: Duke Ellington, lullaby; Ferde Grofe, march; Peter DeRose, waltz; Harry Warren, barcarolle; Lou Alter, serenade; Dana Suesse, nocturne; Sigmund Romberg, humoresque; Morton Gould, caprice; and Vernon Duke, a song without words.

Willson had the number one song in the country and was musical director for the number one radio show. With all the success showering down on him, he still took every opportunity on the air to give a plug to his old hometown, Mason City, Iowa. In his homespun, folksy way, he let the rest of the nation see that he treated ole Squiz Hazleton and Mr. Vance at the music store and Marjorie Sale, who lived next door when he was growing up on Superior Avenue, with the same kind of respect that he showed for Clark Gable, Spencer Tracy, and Fanny Brice—and all of the other Hollywood bigwigs who were making appearances on his show. The old hometown showed its appreciation in numerous ways, some of which amused its most famous son. The *Good News* hour was unabashedly called *The Meredith Willson Hour* in the *Mason City Globe-Gazette*.

Willson's ability to concentrate on whatever he was working on, shutting everything else off from his concentration, allowed him to work on several projects simultaneously simply by shifting mental gears. During the time that he was vamping and leading the orchestra on *Good News* and writing what would become the number one song in the country, he was also composing the musical score for a movie. The music he was scoring was being written for the greatest comedic actor of his day—Charlie Chaplin. Once again, Willson associated himself with greatness, just as he had in his youth when he worked for Sousa and Toscanini, and played scales for Dr. deForest.

Chaplin was regarded as an almost flawless physical comedian, a master at pantomime and sight gags, two skills that made him the undisputed king of comedy in silent movies. Not surprisingly, he resisted the movie industry's transition to "talkies." Born in England in 1889 to show business parents who did not earn much money, Chaplin emigrated

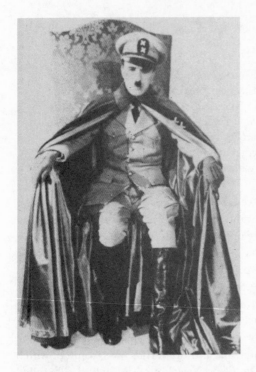

Charlie Chaplin as Adolf
Hitler in his controversial
movie *The Great Dictator.*
MCPLA

to the United States in 1910
and at the age of 21 formed
his own film company. For
the next two decades he made
movies that made his
audiences laugh—and also
think about some of the
ironies, inconsistencies, and
injustices that put scars on the
human soul. Chaplin rose to
stardom in 1914 with *The
Tramp,* in which he pranced
around, pantomimed, and
did pratfalls wearing a derby
hat, a coat two sizes to small,
and pants several sizes too large. His character was simultaneously funny
and yet somehow sad and thought- provoking. It was the signature role of
Chaplin's entire career. He recreated it several times, first in the 1920
movie *The Kid,* again in *The Gold Rush* five years later, and in two movies
with sound, *City Lights* in 1931 and *Modern Times* in 1936. Chaplin
steadfastly refused to move forward with the industry and make movies in
which his audience could hear the characters speak. To Chaplin's way of
thinking, it was demeaning. In 1929 Chaplin, the veteran of almost 40
films, declared, "Talkies are spoiling the oldest art in the world—the art of
pantomime. They are ruining the great beauty of silence. They are
defeating the meaning of the screen."

So it was with a great deal of fanfare in 1940 that Chaplin broke with
the past and decided to make a talkie, and a controversial one at that. As
The Great Dictator was being made, Adolph Hitler's Wehrmacht and
Luftwaffe were marching and bombing their way through Belgium and
France after their stunning success in Poland. Within a year, the war would
expand and draw America into its grasp with Japan's sudden attack at Pearl
Harbor on December 7, 1941.

By this time Chaplin was writing, producing, and directing his own
films for a movie company he co-owned, United Artists. He may have been

a johnny-come-lately, but he became a powerful force in movies with sound just as he had been on the silent screen. And with the entire world on the brink of a catastrophic war, he created *The Great Dictator* with himself in the title role playing a man, who at one point in the movie, bats a replica of the world around in the air as a child might with a toy balloon. Chaplin, who had total control over everything in the production, chose Meredith Willson to score the music for his first "talkie."

Chaplin had heard Willson's "Missions of California" symphony and liked it so well that he wanted to meet the musician and line him up for the movie project. It turned out to be more of a collaboration than purely a Willson composition because of Chaplin's overbearing presence in everything involved in the movie. Despite Chaplin's meddling hand, the Mason City native came away from the experience impressed with everything except Chaplin's world view. The star had never become an American citizen and vowed never to do so. He was, explained Chaplin, an "international citizen," a term that the patriotic Willson found difficult to understand.

Chaplin made it hard for cast and crew to arrange a set work schedule because he was so unpredictable. Sometimes he would work an 18-hour day and expect everyone else to do the same. Other times, he didn't show up to work at all, leaving everyone else hanging around unsure of how to proceed. "Charlie has no idea of time," Willson once explained. "Once he knocked off work at the studio in the afternoon, arranged for the next day's shooting and went home. He came back exactly one month later. Everyone else reported for work every day, but Charlie didn't show up. Toward the end, people began to get to work late, and when he did arrive, on the dot at nine o'clock, he was terribly perturbed because the technicians and actors weren't there on time," he said.

Willson thought Chaplin rather selfish and inconsiderate, but he also said he was a great artist and that he learned a lot from him. He watched as Chaplin took a sound track, cut it in fragments, and taped it back together, getting just the sound he wanted. One scene was shot before Willson was scheduled to be on the set. Chaplin, who had the dual role of dictator and barber in the movie, was shaving a customer in the scene that was already finished. He was supposed to do it to the music of a Brahms number, done by an orchestra conducted by Willson. But to get it over with and go on to other work, the scene was shot with phonograph music playing in the background. It became Willson's job to fit the music of the orchestra to Chaplin's every movement, which was already filmed. It was a daunting task for a hard taskmaster.

Willson planned to do it slowly and carefully, a few measures at a time, so that it would be done correctly the first time. He told his orchestra members to plan on taking two weeks to complete it. On a Monday morning, the work was about to begin. Willson suggested that the orchestra run through the entire scene, just so members would know what they were up against in trying to time their music to every action in the scene. Chaplin, who was always around, suggested that the run-through be filmed, in case any of it would be useable. Willson motioned with his baton, the cameras rolled, and the orchestra played. When they were done, Chaplin laid face down on the stage, shouting "that's it, that's it." Like a champion Olympic gymnast, Willson's orchestra had "stuck" the landing on its first try.

Many of the music plans between Chaplin, Willson, and the orchestra members were made at Chaplin's house with Chaplin, and not Willson, calling the shots. The musicians became more like musical secretaries, quickly writing things down as Chaplin dictated. He would hum a tune or sit down and play it at the piano, just the way he wanted it in the movie. It was up to Willson and the orchestra members to do it the way Chaplin wanted it done. He would often describe what he wanted by mentioning a particular composer. "Do it more Chopin style," he would say.

The Great Dictator featured an all-star cast. Chaplin had contracted veteran screen performers (and his wife) Paulette Goddard, Jack Oakie, Reginald Gardiner, Henry Daniell, and Billy Gilbert. The final version, after all of the editing, lasted two hours and seven minutes, incredibly long for a picture of that era—especially one from a man who had thumbed his nose at the whole concept of "talkies" just a few years earlier. The movie and those who made it were nominated for several Academy Awards, including Willson for best original score, but came up empty on Oscar night.

Willson's next movie experience came the following year when Samuel Goldwyn hired him to do the music for *The Little Foxes*, a compelling drama about a southern family dealing with the social adjustments of the Reconstruction era. This one was not a one-man show but the collaborative effort of some Hollywood heavyweights. It was produced by Goldwyn and directed by William Wyler, based on a screenplay by Lillian Hellman who wrote the original play.

Wyler was a German-born director who teamed with Goldwyn on ten motion pictures, including *Jezebel, Wuthering Heights,* and two Academy Award winners, *Mrs. Minniver* and *The Best Years of Our Lives.* The stars of *The Little Foxes* were Bette Davis, Herbert Marshall, Teresa Wright, Richard Carlson, and Dan Duryea. The main man, the man everyone had to please was Goldwyn himself, who was a bit of an eccentric. Eccentricity was part of his image, but that image was legend in Hollywood. Goldwyn is credited with such classic lines as "include me out," and "I can tell you in two words im-possible," both of which Willson thought could have been the work of a clever press agent. But, then again, maybe not. Willson delighted in relating the story about the time he was in Goldwyn's office and his secretary asked if she could throw away some materials from his overflowing file cabinets. He told her she could, but to be sure to keep copies of everything she threw away.

Willson's moving spiritual, "Never Feel Too Weary to Pray," barely escaped being edited out of the one hour and 55 minute film. The song not only landed an Oscar nomination for its composer, but became Willson's third hit single in as many years.

Willson was now well established as one of America's most gifted orchestra leaders and composers, and his on-the-air buffoonery—the stuff he was warned years ago not to do—had helped catapult him into the limelight as one of the nation's most popular entertainers. He was also a great storyteller, and millions loved tuning in to listen to him. Willson not only enjoyed writing songs about romantic relationships, he liked to have some fun talking about them too.

He had a theory as a teenager that a man and woman who had never met could develop an instant romantic connection just by making eye contact, and that connection would be strong enough that they would kiss without either one of them saying a word or offering any resistance. He said that many years later, he got the chance to test his theory in a train station in Pittsburgh. He was sitting on a bench in the station, waiting for a train to take him back to New York when he noticed an attractive woman sitting on a bench across from him. He said they exchanged several glances over a period of about half-an-hour and neither seemed to mind the attention. When her train pulled up and she got on, Willson jumped aboard. Without a word he sat down and kissed her, got up, got off, and just made it to his train which had pulled up on another track. As the trains steamed off their separate ways, the last image he had of the woman was of her smiling at him. He didn't know her name and they never spoke during the brief encounter. It was another example of the Willson bravado that Alzonzo and John would have appreciated—having the courage to try and not be afraid of being embarrassed by the results.

Willson, always the romanticist, gave the following advice in 1938 on how young women could use phonograph music to woo their boyfriends:

> For the strong, awkward suitor who is always knocking over the fish bowl, play him something like Delibes' 'Pizzacato Polka' or Chaminade's 'Scarf Danee.' The chances are he's inhibited with thoughts of butterflies and morning dew on honeysuckle.
>
> The wistful, Eau de Cologne is a sucker for stirring melodies like 'Anchors Aweigh' or 'United States Field Artillery March.' It makes him think he's a martinet. If he's downright artistic, he's apt to respond to Delius' 'First Cuckoo in Spring.'
>
> Then there is the bookworm or professorial type. He can be pried out of his lethargy by a song a little to the ribald side. 'Frankie and Johnnie' ought to knock him loose from his glasses.
>
> A Tarzan immediately feels the need to defend fair womanhood upon hearing an old-fashioned gallop like 'Light Calvary Overture.' Whether you're fair or dark makes no particular difference.
>
> For the mamma-boy type who is always homesick, I suggest a series of sea chanties. After listening to something like 'What Do You Do With a Drunken Sailor?' he'll be so grateful he's not on sea that he'll be grateful.
>
> For businessmen: Perk him up with a tune like 'Cuddle Up a Little Closer.' Businessmen like that one whether they're tired or not.
>
> Traveling Salesmen: Close all the windows and play Strauss' 'Dance of Salome' over and over again.
>
> Firemen: Something like 'I'm An Old Cowhand' but never, never 'Hands Across the Table.' If you do, he'll bolt out of the room and come back with the elevator man and the janitor to start a four-handed pinochle game.
>
> Gigilos: First time out, play ' I Can't Give You Anything But Love, Baby.' If he comes back the second time, you know you've got him hooked.
>
> Sailors: Reach up on the rack and pull down any record. If he's still shy, play him 'Minnie the Mermaid.' It'll show him your credulous about the tall tales he'll tell you after the honeymoon."

Many newspapers played the story of Willson's advice as if it was the straight scoop. His hometown *Globe-Gazette* headlined it, "Meredith Willson Gives Advice to Amateur Sirens; Former Mason Cityan Now Supplying Melodies for Snappy Love Scenes." The much larger and not-so-local *St. Louis Star-Times* gave the story a headline reading "Musical Director Advises Amateur Sirens on Getting Their Man."

It was not the first nor would it be the last time Willson would have a little fun with his audience.

Meredith Willson, the military music man, inscribed and mailed this photograph to his brother Cedric in January of 1943. *MCPLA*

Chapter 6

"Whether or not they sell Ford cars, the talk, the music and the People keep Willson the busiest star on the summer air—which probably also was his idea."

— *Newsweek*

Not Every Song is a Hit

*D*eeply embroiled in World War II, America needed men and women to serve overseas as well as back home, where they would work overtime to keep up the morale and patriotism. Officials in the War Department called Meredith Willson.

They knew he had an unmatched track record in radio, not only for directing music but for writing it. It was also common knowledge that Willson could quickly write a good piece of music about any subject. It was not unusual for him to sit down at a piano and write the music and lyrics to a song in the space of a couple of hours.

"Can you write one for the civilian truck drivers?" asked the voice on the phone.

"Yes," was Willson's simple and self-assured reply. Like most Americans, Willson wanted to do whatever he could for the war effort; if writing music was his contribution, that was fine with him.

Within a few hours he produced a little ditty called "My Ten-Ton Baby and Me," and sent it off in the mail the next day. A few months later, Willson received a copy of a truckers magazine in the mail. There, on one of the back pages, was a reprint of his song. And that was the last that anybody heard of it.

Before long the USO called asking for a song in tribute to its volunteers. Willson responded with "Gangway, You Rats, Gangway," which unfortunately had about the same staying power as "Ten-Ton Baby and Me."

The next phone call came from someone affiliated with the WACs (Women Air Corps), asking for a song to highlight that unit's efforts. No problem, said Willson, and within a few hours he composed "Yankee Doodle Girl." A lieutenant in the WACs had also written a piece for the organization, and the top brass selected it as their official song. No matter, thought Willson. There would be other songs to write for the war effort.

"Fire Up—Carry On to Victory" was the result of a request for a tune for the Chemical Warfare Division. But, like his "Yankee Doodle Girl" for the WACs, it too came to nothing. Willson learned within a week or two that a song penned by an enlisted member of the division had been selected to embody the spirit of the Chemical Warfare Department. Still another opportunity came along, and he wrote a piece for the cavalry called "Hit the Leather." It was never used.

Willson tried not to be discouraged by this string of musical flops. One night, shortly after his latest rejection, he and friend Bernie Milligan decided to stop in a burlesque house in San Diego. On stage was a bevy of strippers strutting their stuff—to the music of "Gangway, You Rats, Gangway!" Strippers dancing in San Diego to music he had written free for his country comprised the height of his "success" in writing music for the war effort.

The very next day Willson tried to serve his country another way: he enlisted in the Army. Not surprisingly, the composer was assigned to the Armed Forces Radio Service. AFRS handled the production of overseas radio broadcasts, most of which were entertainment programs performed by Hollywood stars in front of live audiences. A modern-day comparison would be the annual Jerry Lewis Telethon for Muscular Dystrophy, where one entertainer after another comes on in an effort to rally the troops for a worthy cause. The big difference was that the AFRS programs were performed daily.

Not every show included live entertainment. Many consisted of taped music fed into the programs, which in turn meant more work for Willson, since he was responsible for providing the music. By 1944, the indefatigable musician was helping with 126 programs a week, including many popular regular shows like Mail Call, At Ease, Jubilee, and Front Line Theater. They were recorded before live audiences and played for troops on the front lines throughout the islands of the Pacific, in Burma, China, Italy, France, and even Alaska.

One of the most popular AFRS shows was called *Command Performance* because it drew some of Hollywood's top performers. One of its broadcasts made show business history when Bob Hope, Frank Sinatra, and Bing Crosby all performed on the same stage together for the first time. A *Command Performance* classic was the 90-minute Dick Tracy show—a hilarious takeoff on the popular cartoon program. Its star-studded cast included Bing Crosby as Dick Tracy, Dinah Shore as Tess Truehart, Frank Sinatra as Shaky, Bob Hope as Flat-top, Jimmy Durante as the Mole, Judy Garland as Snowflake, and Frank Morgan as Vitamin Flintheart. Even the Andrews Sisters were on the show. A thoroughly delighted Willson led the orchestra.

The show opened with Harry Von Zell, who would later gain fame as the announcer for the George Burns and Gracie Allen radio and television programs, proclaiming: "Command Performance USA, presented by the Armed Forces Radio Services this week and every week until it's over, over there." At that instant Willson's musicians broke in with a stirring few bars of George M. Cohan's World War I-era classic, "Over There."

Von Zell resumed his narrative: "Now it's come to our attention that a lot of you guys have been reading comic books while our shows are on. We realize that you men and women in the Army, Navy, Coast Guard and Marines can do exactly as you please at any time," at which point Von Zell stopped and giggled, prompting the audience to do the same.

"But," he continued, "*Command Performance* hates to lose any listeners—so for you guys who like comic strips, tonight we're going to devote our entire time to the super-duper, two-fisted, he-man thriller, one of your real favorites, Dick Tracy."

"So now it's on to the first comic strip operetta of all time, 'Dick Tracy in b Flat, or Isn't He Ever Going to Marry Tess Trueheart?'"

Von Zell's opening was followed by a production number, directed by Willson and sung by the entire cast. At this point Bing Crosby, as the love struck Dick Tracy, inaugurated a bit of ridiculous dialogue guaranteed to draw laughs:

"Ah, this is the house and this is Tess Trueheart's window. Would that I be a bird so that I could perch upon her sill. . ." By this time, two minutes into the show, the audience was rolling in laughter.

Crosby then crooned a love song and knocked on Tess's door. Dinah Shore, playing Tess, responded in song: "Who's that knocking on my door? Who's that singing through my door? Bringing songs to my boudoir. . ."

Crosby broke in, singing jubilantly, "It is I—Dick Tracy," bringing more laughter from the audience.

Tess continued her song:

"How I love your square-cut chin, I'll come down and let you in."

(Footsteps can be heard on a stairway.)

"Hi ya, Dick, give me some skin. . ."

Crosby broke in, crooning, "Thank you skads, Tess Trueheart," and the audience laughed again.

Crosby, Shore, Hope, Sinatra and the others made their way through their lines, occasionally ad-libbing and constantly trying to restrain themselves from breaking into uncontrolled laughter. Willson, who had seen and done a lot of radio shows in his day, called this one of the greatest programs in the history of radio broadcasting.

Willson spent his entire three years with the Armed Forces Radio Service in Hollywood. Although he never left southern California during his World War II service, he faced the same plight most GI's confronted when the war was over: he needed a job.

Just about that time, Burns and Allen, one of the hottest comedy teams in radio, needed a musical director and someone who could serve as a foil for many of the jokes on their program. Once again, Willson's ability to act both the stooge and serious musician paid off. And his career had come full circle. Burns and Allen were sponsored by Maxwell House, the company he worked for on Showboat, and their announcer was Von Zell, the same announcer he worked with on Command Performance.

The Burns and Allen team was one of the most successful in the history of show business. Their radio program had been on the air continuously since 1933 under a variety of names. At the height of their radio and stage popularity in 1949, the couple made a successful transition into television. The basic premise of the show was any storyline that could work around Burns and Allen comedy sketches. There were songs and even some occasional vaudeville routines.

The deadpan Burns was the perfect foil for his wife, who would prattle on about a problem and in the process get her facts thoroughly confused. Eventually she reached a conclusion that sounded reasonable to her, but

George Burns and Gracie Allen had one of the hottest radio programs on the air when Meredith Willson was invited to join the show as musical director and comedic foil. *MCPLA*

based on her faulty thought process. The audience loved it. A typical Gracie moment went something like this:

"Did you know that the police in Los Angeles were looking for a New York madman?" she asked. "You'd think in a city this size, they could find one of their own!"

George, of course, would agree with that assessment—and the audience would explode in laughter, week after week.

Willson joined the successful show in 1945. In addition to acting as its musical director, he was George and Gracie's tenant and next door neighbor. The composer gave his hometown a plug in the opening moments of the first episode, as Gracie was meeting her new neighbor.

"Willson's my name; Meredith Willson. I'm from Mason City, Iowa," he said.

"Isn't it a small world?" replied Gracie. " I was born in San Francisco, California, right in the same country."

The first show incorporated Willson's roots into the storyline. His character had moved in next door as a tenant of George and Gracie—without George knowing it. Gracie and Willson were trying to figure out how he could make a good impression on grouchy George.

"If I was back in Mason City, Iowa," he said, "I would take food over to the new neighbor." When Gracie told him that would work with George, Willson went back to his apartment and fixed a meal for him. George, however, entered the apartment, saw the food on the table, and thought his old tenant—the one he had kicked out—hadn't left! At the same time, Willson emerged from another room and saw George, whom he mistook for the same old tenant. After a few words the two got into a tussle that climaxed with Willson breaking his flute over George's head. The show closed with all of the confusion finally cleared up and Gracie advising Willson, "Go buy another flute—and sell your old one to Guy Lombardo."

Willson, by now a full-fledged Hollywood star, delighted the home folk with his frequent mentions of Mason City. Another instance of this occurred on a show called *Star of Stars*, a program where sponsors paraded their top talent for the new season up to the microphones to do a sketch or two. In one of the bits, Willson tried to persuade bandleader Ozzie Nelson and his wife, Harriet, to buy a radio from him.

"This radio is so unique," he bragged, "it can pick up the local radio station in Mason City, Iowa." When he tried to demonstrate it for the skeptical couple, however, he tuned in the Chicago Cubs–St. Louis Cardinal baseball game from St. Louis.

"Whoops, wrong number," joked Willson.

At the end of the season, George and Gracie asked Willson to be their summer replacement. It was, in essence, a chance for him to have his own show. Willson put together a low-budget, mostly music production that made its debut on June 6, 1946. It was not a rousing success. According to the Hooper ratings—which were gospel to the sponsors in those days—not many people listened to it. But Canada Dry, the ginger ale people, liked it enough to sponsor the show for the fall season. His own show on prime time radio! It was yet another first for Willson.

The name of the show was changed to *Sparkle Time*—a reminder not only of the talent on the show but of the fizz of the sponsor's beverage. It remained on the air for two years under Canada Dry sponsorship. When new sponsors came on, the show's name was changed to *Meredith Willson's Music Room*, and hung on for two more years.

Willson's show is best remembered not for the music-comedy-talk format that was now a longstanding staple in radio, but for its commercials. Willson developed a unique approach to support his sponsors. His vocal group consisted of two women and three men. In order to give the ads a little different flavor, something that might grab the attention of the audience, Willson decided to have his group announce the commercials in unison. They practiced on simple ditties like "Mary Had a Little Lamb" until the five were so perfect in their delivery that they sounded like one person. Once that was mastered, Willson took them to the next level by having them sing the words to the commercials in unison. That was the basis for his "Talking People," the rather unimaginative name that somehow caught on with the public, sponsors, and even media critics who were impressed with the concept and its results.

Although the commercials were getting rave reviews, the show itself wasn't getting much attention. When Canada Dry bowed out, Ford Motor Company picked up the show for the following season to help give some zing to its slogan, "There's a Ford in Your Future." The automaker thought the best way to give their slogan the sizzle it wanted was for Willson's "Talking People" to say it in unison, and often. And they did.

Newsweek magazine called it the most unusual commercial gimmick since Lucky Strike had auctioneers do the sales pitch for its cigarettes. "Willson's brainstorm is 'talking people'—five voices that speak as one," the magazine proclaimed:

> Willson leads them the same way he leads his orchestra, with a baton. Starting out as a lively conversation between Willson and the People on some such subject as last week's 'Do you like corn?' the commercial is gradually and adroitly switched by Willson to the subject of cars. That such a commercial is ear catching was proved last April when Willson and the People were selling Canada Dry Ginger Ale—and New York City College voted theirs the best ad gimmick in radio. Both the show and the People are Willson's idea.
>
> Whether or not they sell Ford cars, the talk, the music and the People keep Willson the busiest star on the summer air—which probably also was his idea.

Radio was still wildly popular, but the relatively new medium of television was beginning to siphon off most of the new ideas rolling down the pike. It was also taking many of radio's top performers with it.

Meredith and Rini strike a Hollywood publicity pose. The pair performed together on television and in concert on college campuses across the country. *Mason City Globe-Gazette*

Chapter 7

"If I can capture just 10 percent of the qualities of my wife, I'll have marvelous material for a Broadway musical."
— *Meredith Willson*

Rini

The news dispatch from California on March 5, 1947 was simply unbelievable:

> HOLLYWOOD (AP) – Meredith Willson, music composer and director, Tuesday was divorced by Mrs. Elizabeth Willson on grounds of mental cruelty. They were married 26 years ago in Albert Lea, Minn., and separated last July. Under a property settlement approved by the court, Mrs. Willson will receive approximately 25 percent of the musician's earnings, a Beverly Hills home, a gasoline station in San Francisco, $27,500 in bonds, $25,000 insurance and some securities. Mrs. Willson testified her husband stayed out late and went on prolonged trips and answered evasively when she tried to learn where he had been.

The famous couple portrayed to the public as having one of Hollywood's happiest marriages had separated one month before their

26th wedding anniversary in 1946. Their marriage ended the way it started, suddenly, and without much explanation.

Peggy Willson, who never attempted to share the spotlight with her famous husband, lived an apparently quiet, comfortable life after their divorce. On November 10, 1950, she married LeRoy Allison Van Bomel, a wealthy eastern businessman and president of the National Dairy Products Association. He was one month shy of his 65th birthday; she was 49.

In the vast Willson archives housed at the Mason City Public Library, where several volumes of official records, newspaper and magazine articles, photographs, and other memorabilia are stored, there is but one thin file folder on the life of Peggy Willson. The sum total of its contents include Peggy's handwritten note to someone concerning an upcoming doctor's appointment, a dairy association booklet containing a photo of her second husband, and a receipt from Elmwood Cemetery, Mason City, with the notation, "no final date on the marker." Meredith Willson wrote three autobiographical books, each brimming (as one might expect) with personal details of his life. Just as he never mentioned his parents' divorce in any of them, he also never mentioned Peggy, his wife and confidant of 26 years.

Meredith and Peggy apparently never had any personal contact again. Twenty-three years after their divorce on August 20, 1970, a courier from a florist delivered roses to Peggy at her home in New York. She must have been surprised when she opened them and discovered the identity of the sender. The flowers were from Meredith on what would have been their 50th wedding anniversary, the day the happy youngsters had dashed off to Albert Lea, Minnesota, said their vows, and headed to New York to start their life together.

There is no record of whether she ever acknowledged the gesture.

Eleven months after the divorce, on March 13, 1948, Willson married Ralina Zarova, a Russian-born opera singer nicknamed "Rini" (pronounced Reeni). Like Meredith, she had also been married once before. Both Cedric and Dixie Willson attended the marriage ceremony with Cedric serving as his brother's best man. The new Mrs. Willson wore a bracelet that had once belonged to Meredith's own mother, Rosalie, complete with her initials "R.W." engraved in it. They were the bride's initials as well.

Shortly after he and Rini were married, Willson described the attributes of his new wife. Rini, he announced, believed that a wife should

Meredith and Rini seem to have different reactions as they join the crowd to watch part of a North Iowa Band Festival parade. *Mason City Globe-Gazette*

live for her mate and do for him as Priscilla did for John Alden. He said Rini shined and buffed his shoes every day before he left the house—and while he was wearing them. She also thought that the household and all of its activities, including answering the phone, were the wife's responsibility because it was all a part of her belief that the husband's happiness came first.

In addition to her obvious adoration for Meredith, Rini had show business pizzaz that complimented her husband's. The Willsons once threw a lavish cocktail party at their Los Angeles home for a guest list that included many Hollywood stars as well as members of the press. Ben Gross of the *New York Daily News* reported on it for his readers:

> Guests flock into the music room. Edwin MacArthur, the noted opera and symphony conductor, is at the piano. Beside him in an eye-catching crimson lace cocktail gown stands Meredith's beautiful wife, Rini. 'She's going to sing a `Mimi' aria from LaBoheme,' Willson whispers. 'But Rini is somewhat rusty on her Italian words Watch now—whenever she forgets, Mac will throw her the lines.'
>
> "And that's exactly what Mac does, prompting her occasionally in perfect Italian. Rini sings Mimi's lilting outburst with lyrical beauty and dramatic fervor. Her pure tones are so exquisitely uttered that the crowd breaks into bravos. Everyone agrees that Meredith's wife would be as much of a success on radio and TV as she had been in west coast opera. Then someone suggests the singing of 'You and I,' the title of one of Meredith's many hit songs. He replaces MacArthur at the piano and Rini swings into the gay popular number.

Ralina Zarova Willson was born in Russia in 1912. Her father was Russian, her mother French. Rini studied dance and music as a child and first went on stage at age seven. She came to the United States with her family in 1927, and her show business career started with appearances in clubs and concerts as a singer and dancer. Rini had a big, bold soprano voice that boomed out an octave higher than most other singers could achieve. She appeared in a play called "Mistress of the Inn" in 1935 and was spotted by an NBC talent scout who signed her to appear in network radio shows. One of her conductors on those shows in the early 1940s was Meredith Willson.

After they were married, one of the first trips the couple undertook was a return to Mason City, Iowa, to participate in its North Iowa Band Festival Parade, a spectacular annual musical event whose highlight was a parade featuring dozens of regional high school bands and floats. The Willsons rode in the back of an open convertible down Federal Avenue, waving to the thousands of people lining the streets to see their hometown hero and his new wife. (Willson had missed the 1947 festival the year of his divorce from Peggy.) When he arrived for the festival in 1948 with his new wife

Meredith and Rini Willson enjoying the adoring hometown crowd on band festival day. It was the first opportunity for Meredith's hometown to meet his new wife. MCPLA

Rini—in his first wife's hometown—many, including Rini and Meredith, wondered how the small town would receive her. As it turned out, they had little to worry about. Rini won over Mason Cityans with her vivacious personality, her cheery "Hello, Ioway" uttered in her unique high-pitched voice and distinct, but not distracting, Russian accent. She was "a stunning brunette in a dark blue spangled dress," reported the *Mason City Globe-Gazette.*

Willson and Rini traveled together extensively and did musical shows in arenas all over the country. Willson sat at a piano, telling stories about growing up in Iowa, and singing his songs. Rini would stand at his side, sometimes joining him in a duet, sometimes breaking into a solo, her voice projecting boldly, an engaging and infectious smile spreading from ear to ear.

She also appeared in three television specials Meredith hosted for CBS in the summer of 1964. One reviewer described the couple as "homespun hokum and continental charm." Rini had a way of twisting the English language that amused not only her husband but the American public as

Meredith and Rini. He said he wanted to write a play about her someday and that if he could embody one-tenth of her enthusiasm in it, the play would be a success. *MCPLA*

well. She would say things like "he sprained his uncle" and don't park next to a "fire hydrogen." She gets particularly upset, she said, when critics referred to her husband as a "country pumpkin."

Rini said some marriages survive when husband and wife lead different lives and therefore enjoy the brief times they have together. Her marriage, she explained, was just the opposite. "It's wonderful when married people share the same interests, but we carry it even further. I audition all of Meredith's songs and we always go on tour together."

On one 1964 tour, however, the couple was forced to split up when Rini was stricken with a bad cold in Arizona. She flew back to Hollywood to recuperate, leaving her husband to do a solo performance in Tucson that night. During the show he fell off the stage and into the orchestra pit—the only time in his career that an accident like that ever happened. Meredith was not injured but he was deeply embarrassed, a condition that he had learned to handle all the way back to his days with Sousa.

"We agreed it was an evil omen," said Rini, whose many interests included astrology. "So, cold or no cold, I came hurrying back."

Rini said she could always tell when her husband was nervous during a rehearsal because he drank a lot of water. She described one of their television specials together as a "17-cup show." Willson dedicated one of his books "to my Rini," and even envisioned writing a Broadway show about her. "If I can capture just 10 percent of the qualities of my wife, I'll have marvelous material for a Broadway musical," he said.

Meredith is all smiles as he works on a manuscript on the manual typewriter in his study in Los Angeles. Willson wrote 400 songs in his career and wrote or collaborated on three Broadway shows—and one other that never made it to Broadway. *MCPLA*

Chapter 8

"Nothing prepares you for Broadway."
— *Meredith Willson*

The Bucolic Philosopher and the Big Show

*I*n the late 1940s and early 1950s, the momentum of the electronic media in America shifted quickly from radio to television—and it swept many of radio's brightest stars along with it. Burns and Allen made the switch after their 1949 radio season. Willson stayed with radio but left the Burns and Allen show at the start of the 1949 fall season. He hosted two other shows, one sponsored by Ford Motor Company and the other by Jell-O.

The sponsors were not as interested in the shows for their content as much as the clever commercials Willson devised. Both radio programs originated on the East coast and were rebroadcast on the West coast three hours later. Ironically, a series of transmission mistakes on both shows cut out the commercials from the West coast broadcasts—the very shows the big brass from Ford and General Foods (Jell-O's parent company) had tuned in to hear.

Neither show lasted more than one year, but Jell-O provided Willson with two more firsts in his career. He wrote his first commercial jingle for the company (sung naturally enough by "The Talking People"), and Jell-O gave him his first shot at television. The company sponsored The Meredith Willson Show, a half-hour variety program that was shoved into the summer schedule to replace another program that had been taken off the air.

Unfortunately, there is not much information available today about *The Meredith Willson Show*. It debuted on July 31, 1949, and its last episode was telecast just a few weeks later on August 21. The show ran on NBC from 8:30 to 9:00 p.m. on Sunday nights. Other than Meredith, there was only one other regular performer on the show, a singer named Norma Zimmer who later gained fame as band leader Lawrence Welk's "Champagne Lady." Willson later groused that the budget for the show was so low that if he wanted to use any props, he had to bring them from home. Still, the program earned a good review from Harriet Van Horne in the *New York Daily Telegram*. Van Horne, who had criticized Willson's radio antics in the past, liked the television show but warned her readers that Willson was still a "bucolic philosopher." He still "refers to Mason City, Iowa, at every possible opportunity."

At the same time that NBC was making great strides in television, the network was still holding out hope that radio variety shows were not dead. It threw a lot of time, effort, and money into one called *The Big Show*, hoping listeners would agree with the title. Tallulah Bankhead, an aging Alabama-born actress with a gravel voice, sharp tongue, and instant name recognition, was the hostess. Willson was hired as the show's musical director. Bankhead, who called everybody "dahling," enjoyed a long show business career both in film and on stage. She won the New York Film Critics Award in 1944 for her work in Alfred Hitchcock's film *Lifeboat*. Bankhead was best known, however, for her work in plays such as Lillian Hellman's *The Little Foxes*, and Thornton Wilder's *The Skin of Our Teeth*, for which Wilder was awarded the Pulitzer Prize and Bankhead the New York Critics Circle Award as best actress of the year.

The Big Show was a weekly, 90-minute extravaganza with stars such as Groucho Marx, Louis Armstrong, Dinah Shore, Bob Hope, Dean Martin and Jerry Lewis, Beatrice Lillie, and whoever else happened to be in town that NBC could corral. It was a peacetime *Command Performance* and NBC's last hurrah in prime-time radio. Once again, Willson was not only the musician but also the wag. One of the show's running gags was Bankhead, in her deep, husky voice, acknowledging everyone on stage and with Willson responding, "Thank you, Miss Bankhead, sir."

The program went on the air for the first time on November 5, 1950. The guests included some top stars, including Jimmy Durante, Jose Ferrer, Paul Lukas, and Danny Thomas. Initially, ratings were high and reviews were good. "It was in practically every respect a perfectly wonderful show—witty, tuneful, surprisingly sophisticated and brilliantly put together," wrote critic John Crosby. Bankhead was impressed when she learned that more people listened to her on one radio broadcast than had seen her in 30 years of stage and screen performances.

The Big Show had some classic moments. Two occurred on the same day. Frank Sinatra, who was slated as the featured guest, called in sick a few hours before air time. He had been scheduled to sing a couple of songs and participate in the sketches, some of which had lines specifically aimed at him. Sinatra's illness created a big hole in a live show and not much time to fix it. There certainly wasn't time to rewrite the entire show. The only solution was to find another singer to fill in and to rewrite the lines aimed at Sinatra. But who would be available on a Sunday afternoon for a show that was to go on the air in just a couple of hours?

The dilemma was solved when one of the show's producers got Frankie Laine, a famous torch singer, to agree to do the show. This meant that none of the "Frankie" jokes had to be rewritten. Because the show was on radio, it was not essential for Laine to memorize his lines. He just needed to read them clearly and on cue.

There was one more problem to resolve. The orchestration for one of the songs was not in Frankie Laine's key or style. By the time that flaw was discovered, there was no time to change it. The song was to be sung in a duet with a young soprano with a good voice but not much show business experience. Willson agreed to fill in and sing the male part of the duet. He had never seen the soprano before and had not been introduced. In fact, he didn't even know her name.

When the show went on, Frankie Laine performed like he had been rehearsing all week and Willson and the soprano made it through their duet without a hitch. In fact, after the show, the young woman's father called to say how much he had enjoyed it. The call came from the White House. The soprano was none other than Margaret Truman, daughter of the president of the United States.

The most rigorous activity for *The Big Show* was its rehearsal schedule, which began at 2:00 p.m. every Sunday afternoon, just four and one-half hours before air time. The late start accommodated guests from Broadway and night clubs who had worked late the night before. Many of them were due back on stage Sunday night just one-half hour after *The Big Show* signed off. Rehearsal time was particularly hectic for Willson because one of the show's gimmicks was to have guests perform musical numbers that were totally out of their venue. One night, for example, comedian Groucho Marx sang "Some Enchanted Evening" in Italian. Another night, Ed Wynn, another comedian, sang what he called an "opera with interruptions." The clever composition had Wynn stopping several times in the middle of his singing to talk to the audience. The difficulty was in the timing: Willson and his orchestra had to start and stop exactly when Wynn did.

NBC went to extraordinary lengths to promote the show, beginning with its 6:30 starting time. At CBS, the popular Jack Benny program began at 7:00. Benny, one of the greatest comedians of all time, had already made the transition to TV, but continued also on radio because of his immense popularity. NBC started *The Big Show* at 6:30 to try to capture some of Benny's audience before his show started, hoping they wouldn't switch over to him at 7:00 p.m. In an unusual move, NBC dispensed with its usual 7:00 p.m. station break to avoid giving listeners an easy opportunity to switch over to Benny.

Another NBC publicity stunt occurred at the start of the program's second season. On September 16, 1951, the show was broadcast live from the Empire Theater in London, giving British fans the opportunity to see Bankhead, who had performed on stage there many times. It also provided American audiences the chance to learn how popular the show was, even outside the United States.

Broadcasting from England was fun for most everyone involved—except Willson, who spent much of his time putting out troublesome fires. His sheet music for the show, for example, was late arriving because it got held up in customs. To give the show a truly international flavor, producers hired 60 French musicians for Willson's orchestra. It was not until the Sunday afternoon rehearsal, however, that Willson discovered that the musicians thought the performance was Sunday afternoon. Most of them had engagements Sunday night and would not be able to appear on the live program. A frantic Willson cajoled and argued with the musicians, who finally agreed to arrange their schedules to return for the taping that evening. The show, starring Bankhead, Allen, Hoffa, and its emotionally exhausted orchestra leader, also featured guest stars Josephine Baker, Gracie Fields, George Sanders, and Joan Fontaine. It went off without a flaw.

Part of the standard fare for the show was for Bankhead to ask her guests to introduce themselves with a brief biography. Thanks to writers such as Goodman Ace, the results were almost always hilarious. For example, the guests introduced themselves this way on a 1952 program:

Phil Foster: "Foster, Phil. Born 1919 in Brooklyn. Died 1951 in the Polo Grounds. Cause of death: Brancitis." (This was a reference to the Brooklyn Dodgers losing the 1951 National League baseball championship to the New York Giants on a home run off of Brooklyn pitcher Ralph Branca—a fact that the howling audience picked up on right away.)

Richard Easton: "Easton, Richard. I began in show business as a spear carrier in *Medea* starring Judith Anderson. One night my spear dipped and I caught her right in the middle of the second act. Miss Anderson never reached greater heights."

Ethel Merman: "Merman, Ethel. After high school, I went to secretarial school where I studied typing, dictation, bookkeeping and wrestling. On my first job as a stenographer, I was invited to a party on Long Island. They asked me to sing and a producer heard me. He was sitting in his office on Forty-Second Street at the time." (Merman was well known for her booming voice.)

Peter Lorre: "Lorre, Peter. I started my career in the theater as a romantic actor but against my will, they put me in horror pictures. I always wanted to be the actor to get the girl, but in my pictures, by the time I get the girl, she's dead."

As *The Big Show* entered its second season, Willson signed on to do a weekly radio program called *Encore*, and a weekly television show called *The Name's The Same.* The two shows fit snugly into his schedule between the Sunday broadcasts of *The Big Show*.

The new radio show Encore was a music program featuring Willson and opera stars Robert Merrill and Marguerite Piazza. *The Name's The Same* was a quiz show, a popular new genre in television. The ABC program was produced by Mark Goodson and Bill Todman, who already had a huge hit on their hands at CBS with *What's My Line?* The idea of *The Name's The Same* was for ordinary people with interesting names to try and stump celebrity panelists attempting to guess their names by asking questions. The contestants had the same name as a famous person, such as George Washington or Clark Gable, or an object, like A. Wheel. The show was hosted by Robert Q. Lewis. Willson was a regular panelist from 1951 to 1953, together with playwright Abe Burrows and actress Joan Alexander.

Despite all the hope, help, and hype mustered by NBC, *The Big Show* lasted a mere two years. Many years later author Gerald Nachman, in an attempt to describe the show's place in radio history, wrote that it was a "failed showbiz blitzkrieg that vainly attempted to out-spectacular television."

One aspect of *The Big Show*, however, proved popular with the viewing public and provided another success for Willson. Every week the program closed with cast members singing Willson's song "May The Good Lord Bless and Keep You." Willson had lifted the well-liked tune from another sign-off delivered many years earlier: Rosalie Willson, Meredith's mother, used to say the same thing to her departing Sunday School students at the First Congregational Church in Mason City. (Another of the show's many gimmicks featured each cast member singing a line of the closing song's lyrics, which made for some strange combinations, i.e., Ethel Merman's booming voice followed by Peter Lorre's, for example.)

Just getting the producers to agree to air the song at all, however, proved difficult. Their first reaction to the tune was that they didn't want a hymn on a popular radio program. Besides, they added, it was too corny—a complaint Willson often heard about his work. Willson's persuasion won out, and they decided to go with it to see how the public reacted. Tallulah Bankhead, Douglas Fairbanks Jr. and Jimmy Durante were the first to sing it on the air. The immediate and overwhelmingly popular response to the lyrics and melody proved Willson right and his producers wrong. Willson wisely recorded it as both a folk tune and a spiritual hymn, and long after *The Big Show* was off the air, people were buying the sign-off song. Within a year, nearly one million records had been sold. Many well-known stars performed it in concert, including Jan Peerce, Ezio Pinza, Gracie Fields, and Blanche Thebom. Churches across the country adopted it as part of their workshop music.

Willson had been in show business, in one form or another, for almost 30 years, and had never experienced anything to compare with the public response to "May the Good Lord Bless and Keep You." For a time he averaged 2,000 fan letters a week. Indeed, the hymn took on a life of its own. One night on *The Big Show*, just for variety, Willson decided to speed up the tempo of the song to give it a slightly different beat. He was deluged with cards, letters, and phone calls telling him to leave it alone. One letter writer told him crisply, "Quit jazzing up that hymn!"

One day Willson was at a radio studio in Manhattan when he received a message to call a phone number in Brooklyn. He did not know anybody at that number, but he dialed it nonetheless. A woman answered and asked, "Is this Meredith Willson?"

"Yes it is," he answered.

"May the good Lord bless and keep you," she said and then hung up.

The American public had clearly assumed ownership of the song, and Willson thought he knew why. "It's not a hymn, it's not hillbilly, it's not pop, but it does for all of them," he said. "It's not like what you hear in church. Not much for quality but sure long on feeling. It was corny but so is home and so are the boys overseas, like the GIs in Korea." And, he added proudly, "It was their most requested song."

By this point in his career Willson was actively reducing his laborious radio schedule in order to dedicate substantial amounts of time trying to figure out what it took to succeed in television. The royalties from his hit song came in especially handy during this period of his life. He had also written his first book. *And There I Stood With My Piccolo*, published in 1948, was a stream-of-conscientiousness autobiography full of memories about his days growing up in Mason City and his early adventures in professional music and show business. Three more books would flow from his pen in the next decade.

It did not take Meredith long to discover that writing books wasn't as easy for him as writing music. He tried twice unsuccessfully to write a book before he succeeded with *And There I Stood With My Piccolo*. In recounting his early attempts at being an author, Willson once again displayed his ability to laugh at himself and to perhaps embellish the story just a little, to insure the laugh.

He said he first thought of writing a book when he was doing The Talking People gimmick on the radio commercials. So he called his book *Talking People*. He said he submitted it to an agent who told him to run it through the typewriter again, add 25,000 words, and take out the references to the Talking People.

That was enough to convince him to drop the project and start a new book. This endeavor was about four men who, while neither famous nor powerful, exerted a major influence on his career. He called it *Four Small People*. According to Willson, he submitted it to his agent who told him to run it through the typewriter again, add 25,000 words, and take out the references to the Four Small People.

When he finally wrote a book suitable for publication, Willson said he thought he had a snappy title in *And There I Stood With My Piccolo* until the day a woman approached him at a book signing and asked whether he was the author of *Is My Piccolo Showing?*

In addition to writing books, Willson was also learning the differences between working in radio and working in television. In the early days of

Rini Willson where she was the most comfortable—at her husband's side. The couple are home visiting Vance's Music Store, one of Meredith's favorite local haunts, during the height of Meredith's radio fame. *MCPLA*

former, everyone on a show dressed as if they were going to the prom, even though their nationwide audience couldn't see them. However, their studio audience—primarily composed of their sponsors—could see them, so they dressed accordingly. In television, however, the audience saw the performers all the time. For Willson, this meant having five tailored suits on hand, going to the barbershop once a week instead of once a month, and visiting the dentist four times a year instead of twice. He often griped about how much more difficult it was to prepare for a television show than for radio. "Beside TV, radio is a cinch, a vacation," he said. "The musician will always be fond of radio," he added. "On radio, music is the star, no matter how many big-name performers are involved. On television, music is a spear-carrier, an extra."

A few years later Willson was trying to make his mark in a new area of entertainment. And he knew it would not be easy. "Nothing prepares you for Broadway," he said. "All those years in radio with some guy holding up an applause card—that isn't show business. You aren't a success in show business until you do something that makes people dig down in their pants pocket and buy a ticket."

Alonzo Willson would have approved of Meredith once again trying to be a settler in new territory. Alonzo had traveled 2,000 miles from Illinois to California, mined gold, conducted business, and made his way back home to Illinois in a mere two years, richer in both treasure and spirit.

It would take his grandson three times that long to strike gold on Broadway.

On the set of *The Music Man*, 1961. From left to right: Robert Preston (as Harold Hill), Ruth Hall, Morton Da Costa (director), W. Earl Hall (editor, *Mason City Globe Gazette*), Shirley Jones (Marian the Librarian), and Meredith Willson.

Mason City Globe Gazette

Chapter 9

"As we began, I felt a thrill of excitement.
At last, here was my big chance."

— *Meredith Willson*

"Who the Hell is Meredith Willson?"

*I*n October of 1950, Les Zachels, music columnist for the *Cedar Rapids Gazette*, the second largest newspaper in Iowa, wrote a column suggesting that the University of Iowa needed a new fight song (the present tune, he complained, was simply too corny). Zachels believed Willson would be the ideal person to write it, even though he had never attended the university. Editorial writers picked up on the idea, and Zachels sent the newspaper clippings to Willson in California.

Within a few weeks Willson had not only written a new song, but had played it for the first time on his national radio program on New Year's Eve, 1950. The new tune made its formal debut in Iowa on February 12, 1951, during the half-time performance at an Iowa-Indiana basketball game. Willson shrugged off compliments about how quickly he had responded to the request. "Getting the idea for something like that is the whole thing," he said. "Then you just sit down and write it."

New projects were always on the horizon. In 1951, Cy Feuer, Ernie Martin, and Frank Loesser approached Willson about the possibility of writing a musical comedy about his beloved Iowa, an idea that wife Rini had already talked to him about many times. Willson found the offer tempting. Martin, Feuer, and Loesser were Broadway veterans who knew a good musical when they saw one. The trio had just combined on the production of *Guys and Dolls*, with Loesser writing the music for the Abe Burrows story and Feuer and Martin producing the Broadway show. It had opened at the 46th Street Theater on November 24, 1950, and was in the midst of its 1,200 performances when the men approached Willson about the Iowa project they had in mind for him.

Part of the intrigue was simply the challenge of it all. Writing a musical comedy about his home state had the potential of being the capstone of a long and remarkable career. On a more basic level, it represented potential income for Willson. Aside from the royalties he garnered from "May the Good Lord Bless and Keep You," his income had been steadily diminishing. Radio was clearly on the decline, and he had yet to make serious inroads into television. In terms of his career, Willson explained that he felt like he had one foot on a departing boat, and the other on a receding dock.

So he agreed to give it a try. The first thing he discovered about writing a play, he said later, was that the first four words are the easiest: "Act One, Scene One." It's the fifth one that's a killer. The man who had written hundreds of songs—many dashed off in the span of a single afternoon—struggled with his first attempt as a playwright. He spent the next several weeks writing thirty essays about his days growing up in Mason City, and from these he developed some twenty songs. The problem was finding a way to put them together cohesively. For a while he toyed with the idea of dropping the play altogether and simply selling the stories and songs separately.

Six months after he began work on his Iowa play, Willson received a call from an agent who had a deal for him that was a "sure thing." A new television quiz show was being planned called *The Big Surprise*. The idea of the show was that contestants would come on, answer a series of questions for prize money, and have the chance to win up to $100,000 if they answered all of the questions correctly. What the show needed, the agent explained, was a master of ceremonies to ask the questions, throw in a little dry humor, and keep the show moving along. Both the show's producers and sponsors thought Willson would be a perfect fit. All he had to do was go through the motions at the audition. It was practically a done deal, the agent assured him.

Willson like the idea. Besides, he wasn't making much progress on his play, and he had wanted a more visible and stronger presence on television than just sitting as a panelist on *The Name's the Same.* In addition, his role as a panelist on that program had given him some insight into how quiz shows operated. Taking on a new show would also generate additional income and possibly lead to something bigger, especially since quiz shows had caught the fancy of the American public. Indeed, the popular format had propelled the careers of many stage and radio performers who went on to become popular television personalities. Groucho Marx, for example, already famous for his Marx Brothers movies and radio appearances, garnered more fame and fans as the witty and suggestive host of *You Bet Your Life.* Newspaper reporter Dorothy Kilgallen and Bennett Cerf, a publisher with Random House books, were much better known as panelists on *What's My Line?* than for their day jobs. Bud Collier was known more for being the host of *Beat The Clock* (and later for his role on a game show called *To Tell The Truth*) than for anything else he ever did in his long career. Johnny Carson, host of the *Tonight* show for 30 years and the best known personality on television during his era, gained recognition on national television in the 1950s as the host of a game show called *Who Do You Trust?* Willson's agent was right. All in all, it seemed a good fit.

In 1950, television's prime-time lineup included a dozen quiz programs: *What's My Line?* and *Take a Chance* on Sunday night; *Who Said That?* on Monday night; *Can You Top This?* and *We Take Your Word* on Tuesday; *Break the Bank* on Wednesday; *Stop the Music* and *Truth or Consequences* and *You Bet Your Life* on Thursday; and *Beat the Clock* and *Twenty Questions* and *Quiz Kids* on Friday. In 1951, three new quiz shows were added to the line-up: *It's News to Me* on Mondays, *What's the Story?* on Tuesdays, and *Strike it Rich* on Wednesdays. (The hottest show on Saturday night was *Your Hit Parade,* television's version of the radio show Willson had created 15 years earlier and for which he received no recognition or income.)

Willson agreed to fly to New York for the audition. He was more than ready to dazzle the audience with some good old-fashioned Iowa humor, which had been rolling off his tongue so easily over the years. He had been criticized by some in the press for his continual references to Mason City. Now he was auditioning for people who wanted him to talk about it. The audition was going to be conducted before a live studio audience with producers and sponsors in attendance. The contestants would be competing for prize money. The only difference between the audition and the real thing was that the audition would not be broadcast. Everything else about it was for real, including the prize money.

Before the show, Willson went over the script with the producers and wanted to know the places in it where he could work in some of his hokey Iowa humor. The producers told him to forget about that, to just say things like "you're right, you're absolutely right." When it was time for the show to start, Willson stood backstage, waiting for the theme music and for him to be introduced. On cue, he took two steps backward and then sprang forward, the method he had been taught to give him the "spring" in his step to walk briskly out on stage. Not much went right after that.

Willson was so focused on saying, "you're right, you're absolutely right," that he said it once when the contestant had given the wrong answer. At another time, he said an answer was wrong when it was actually right. The climax of the show—and one of Willson's biggest mistakes—arrived with the long-awaited $100,000 question. As the sponsors, audience, and contestants held their collective breath, Willson read the answer instead of the question.

His audition had been a disaster, something to which Willson was not accustomed. The embarrassed musician left the studio with Rini by his side. No one said a word to them. Exhausted and humiliated, the couple returned to their hotel room and fell into a deep sleep. The next day, they boarded a plane and flew back to California. They never heard a word from anyone connected with the show. *The Big Surprise* made it on the air briefly in 1955 and 1956—with Mike Wallace, later a correspondent for the popular *60 Minutes* television program, acting as one of its hosts.

Within a short time, however, the Willsons turned the embarrassing episode into something positive: humor. For years following the dreadful audition, Meredith would look at Rini (or visa versa) and say, "You're right, you're absolutely right," five words that never failed to produce raucous laughter. As Rini later pointed out, had the audition gone well and the show succeeded, the course of musical history on Broadway and beyond would have changed. Work on what would eventually be known around the world as *The Music Man* would have, at the very least, been delayed for years—and the play may never have been completed.

Willson returned to California and resumed work on his musical comedy, which he called *The Silver Triangle*. The story was about a traveling con man posing as a band instrument salesman in a small town in Iowa called River City. The fast-talking salesman's plan was to fleece the townspeople in a scam involving the purchase of uniforms and instruments for the children. Instead of completing his ruse and absconding with the money, however, he falls in love with the local librarian. As a subplot,

Willson created a spastic boy in a wheelchair whose daily challenges were part of the story.

Willson's work on his play over the next five years is best described as a labor of love, passion, and obsession. He would rise early, between 3:00 and 4:00 a.m. each morning and begin writing. And rewriting. He survived the long mornings with the help of a diet of vitamin pills, papaya, Sanka, and rye toast. (Willson loved rye or wholewheat bread. Lenore Clifford, a retired Mason City school teacher and principal, was once a waitress at a tea room just east of downtown Mason City. She remembers that Willson came in frequently when he was in town and always ordered his hamburger on whole wheat bread instead of on a bun.) The musician-turned-playwright included a long walk in his rigorous daily routine, beginning promptly at 10:15 a.m. The exercise proved to be as important a part of his day as the Sanka and rye toast.

After he finished his first complete draft, it took weeks for him to tear it apart and completely rewrite it. Much to his dismay, his new version ran three hours and 45 minutes—about two hours too long. Feuer and Martin, fresh from their success with *Guys and Dolls* and *Can Can*, were busy with two new musicals, *The Boy Friend* and *Silk Stockings*. Willson, anxious to show them what he had come up with, flew to New York with Rini. It was the first of many cross-country flights over the next few years and the first of many auditions he and Rini would do, many in the apartments of influential Broadway theater people.

This first audition of *The Silver Triangle* was held in Feuer's apartment. Unlike his disastrous trial by fire for his quiz show emcee position, Willson's effort proved an immediate success: Feuer and Martin liked what they heard. After *The Boy Friend* and *Silk Stockings*, they informed a happy Willson, their next project would be *The Silver Triangle*. Feuer and Martin heaped more good news on Willson when they told him they intended to contact Josh Logan to direct it. Landing someone of Logan's standing and experience would be a real coup. He was a top-notch stage and screen director with *Annie Get Your Gun* in 1946, *Mr. Roberts* in 1948, and *South Pacific* in 1949 to his credit. (The euphoria was short-lived—a frequently recurring circumstance over the next few years. Logan sent word that he was definitely interested, but tied up for at least a year on two new projects, the movies *Bus Stop* and *Picnic*.) Waiting for Feuer and Martin to free themselves of other obligations proved helpful, because it gave Willson the time he needed to pare down *The Silver Triangle* and make some of the changes suggested by Feuer and Martin—one of which had to do with the wheelchair-bound boy. De-emphasize his role, they advised, or the kid would steal every scene and detract from the thrust of the story. The veteran pair also counseled a name change for the play, something better suited to Broadway.

Willson and Rini returned home and soon thereafter left Los Angeles to relax in the mountains outside the growing city. They weren't there long before New York interrupted their retreat. Feuer said he wanted to direct *The Music Man*—the new name chosen for Willson's play—and Martin wanted to help rewrite it.

Silk Stockings opened on Broadway on February 21, 1955, and had a run of 477 performances. The day after it opened in New York, Martin arrived in California, ready to work on *The Music Man*. Nearly a year had passed since Willson and Rini had first auditioned the play in Feuer's apartment.

One of the first things Willson did for Martin was play for him a new song he was working on, "Seventy-Six Trombones" and tell him of some plot changes. Marian the librarian was prim and proper on the outside, he confided, but starving for affection within. Similarly, con man Harold Hill was both flamboyant and lonely. That, Willson explained, was a connection the audience would be able to see and appreciate. Martin loved "Seventy-Six Trombones," but thought the story needed a lot of work—much more than just a simple paring for length. The whole thing would have to be rewritten and the characters redone, he said, because Willson had written a play with music. To Martin's way of thinking, it needed to be a musical comedy.

Willson agreed, and spent the spring and summer rewriting the story of the conniving but lovable con man and small town Iowa. If he thought about it, Willson may have realized that the more things changed, the more they stayed the same. He was, after all, in much the same position as deForest had been 35 years earlier, when a much younger Meredith had played musical scales for him in his stuffy New York apartment while the scientist endlessly tinkered and reworked his project. It was the Thomas Edison lesson all over again: every time you try something that didn't work, you learned something new. When viewed on that basis, Willson was learning a lot.

Willson and Martin spent endless hours discussing how to handle the characters. Should the audience know early on that Harold Hill was a con man, or make it a surprise later in the play? Martin finally convinced Willson to establish the con man premise almost from the beginning, so the audience would realize what was happening and have fun with it. Another critical aspect of the play was how the songs themselves should be handled. Willson reached the conclusion that all the music should grow out of the dialogue. In other words, instead of standing alone as separate entities, each song would be analogous to a conversation, and thus advance the plot. Martin agreed. That decision led to a discussion about rhyming lyrics. People don't speak in rhymes, explained Willson, and if the songs were going to be part of the dialogue, the lyrics had to be realistic.

As the months passed and bills piled up, Willson and Rini derived some income by performing road shows together, singing songs and chatting with the audience. In October of 1955, they were doing a show in Grand Bend, Kansas, when they received a phone call from Feuer and Martin (who always seemed to be together when they called.) *The Music Man*, they informed Willson, had been sold to CBS for $100,000 even though it wasn't yet finished. CBS indicated it might even preempt its popular Sunday night television program, *The Ed Sullivan Show,* to put it on the air. It was wonderful news while it lasted, but it lasted about as long as the earlier idea to have Josh Logan direct *The Silver Triangle*. Within a week, the deal fell through because CBS wanted control over casting, which was unacceptable to Feuer and Martin.

Early in 1956, with Willson still busy rewriting and Feuer and Martin working on other productions, the *New York Times* reported in its theater section that the two producers had put *The Music Man* project on the shelf because of other commitments. It became apparent to Willson that he better try to drum up interest with other producers if *The Music Man* was ever going to see the light of day.

In February, the break he was seeking seemed at hand. Jesse Lasky, a producer from MGM called to tell Willson about an idea he had for a movie. It was about a man forming an All-American band made up of the best musicians from all 50 states. Lasky wanted to make arrangements to actually form such a band to perform in the movie, and he needed a march to use as a finale. He asked Willson to write the march for him. The more the two men talked, the more excited they became about combining their individual ideas into one movie.

Once again, however, reality intervened and the excitement waned in a hurry. Lasky called back just one week later and advised Willson that he had changed his mind. The plan, he said, wouldn't work. But he had a new idea, this one a double feature: *The Music Man* followed by *The Big Brass Band*. Since both men had the same agent from the William Morris agency, they arranged a meeting with the agent, together with other brass from that office. Once again, Willson and Rini found themselves auditioning *The Music Man* to a room largely full of strangers.

"As we began, I felt a thrill of excitement," Willson said later. "At last, here was my big chance. These people would help me. Rini and I were at it for three solid hours, and during all of the time, there wasn't a flicker of a smile, not one sound of laughter. There they sat, poker faced. It was torture for Rini and me. When it was over, the men left without saying anything. It was the most heartbreaking night of my life," recalled Willson.

The dejected musicians flew back to California and Meredith resumed his rewriting chores, thankful that the good Lord was still blessing and keeping him with royalties. Lasky eventually made a documentary on brass bands and got Jimmy Stewart, the famous movie star, to narrate it. The All-American band envisioned by Lasky never blew a note.

In June 1956, Cy Feuer confirmed the earlier *New York Times* story. He paid another visit to Willson in California to officially break off their professional relationship, but wanted to make sure there were no hard feelings. As the two sat in Willson's home, Feuer suggested that Willson call Sol Siegel, producer of the successful movie *Philadelphia Story*, because he thought Siegel would be interested in *The Music Man*. As it turned out, Sigel was indeed interested. Once again Meredith and Rini Willson put on an audition, this time in their own home for Siegel and his wife. The producer loved it and informed the elated Willsons that he would contact Bing Crosby about playing the lead. That exciting angle, however, was another false hope: the star was far too busy to participate. Siegel's people also contacted Ray Bolger, a well-known and talented song and dance man. Bolger's most famous role was his portrayal of the scarecrow in The *Wizard of Oz*. Like Crosby, Bolger was interested but was tied up on other projects for at least a year. The rebuffed Siegel quietly moved on to other ventures, and Willson and his play were left hanging in limbo—again.

In August, Willson and Rini left Los Angeles and drove south to San Diego so Meredith could fulfill a two-week commitment to conduct an orchestra for a big pageant. Willson thought it would be a good opportunity for him to clear his mind, at least temporarily, of all the ups and downs and frustrations of trying to make something of *The Music Man*. While in San Diego he met Franklin Lacey, the pageant's producer. Lacey had a wide range of show business experience, including a stint as stage manager for Ziegfeld shows and hosting his own talk show on the west coast. Inevitably, Willson brought up his latest project. Lacey enthusiastically agreed to help him with it. The two became fast friends, and Willson left San Diego fired up once again about his musical comedy involving a con man, librarian, and spastic wheelchair-bound boy. Unlike all the other producers who had professed support for *The Music Man*, Lacey stuck with Willson through the end of the project, and is even credited with helping write the story.

By now, Willson had been working on *The Music Man* for more than four years. He had what everyone thought was a great opening—a train steaming into River City with singers providing the chug-chug-chug of the locomotive through the staccato rhythm of the lines they were chanting. Forty years later this style would be better known as "rap," but in 1956, it was Willson's concept of talking in rhythm. Willson was also toying with another rhythm song, this one featuring the main character, con man Professor Harold Hill. Hill's theme was that there was trouble in River City—trouble with a capital T that rhymes with P and that stands for pool. It was Willson's way of advancing the plot by showing Hill laying the groundwork he needed to convince the townspeople that they could get their kids out of the sordid pool halls by buying them musical instruments and forming a boy's band. It didn't matter that none of the kids knew how to play the instruments, the professor told them, because he would teach them how with his unique "think" method.

In later years, Willson claimed the song "Trouble" was a turning point for him in *The Music Man* project, because it drew the story and lyrics together in one piece. Forty-four years later in 2000, *The Music Man* roared back to life on Broadway. Lead actor Craig Bierko flew to Los Angeles to audition "Trouble" in front of Rosemary Willson. Bierko wanted her stamp of approval that he was the right man to play Harold Hill. According to Willson's widow, "Trouble" was *the* audition piece, and Meredith had always said that if an actor could do "Trouble," he could do anything else in the play. Of all of the lyrics Willson penned during his 60-year career, he is listed in *Bartlett's Book of Familiar Quotations* but once—for the "there's trouble in River City" lyric.

In November of 1956, producer Ernie Martin, who had begged off *The Music Man* project earlier in the year, flew to California to offer Willson work on a new musical entitled *Indian Joe.* Friends reminded a skeptical Willson that Feuer and Martin had never backed a loser, and urged him to take the job. Willson declined. The last thing he wanted to do was siphon his energy away from *The Music Man.* On a whim, he decided instead to call Kermit Bloomgarden, a man he did not know personally but who had just produced *Most Happy Fella* on Broadway. The music for that play was written by Frank Loesser, a friend of Willson's and one of the people who had convinced him years ago that he should write a play about his Iowa boyhood.

Bloomgarden, 53, was a former certified public accountant who became a manager for Broadway producer Arthur Beckhardt. Bloomgarden had a string of successes to his credit, including *Death of a Salesman* in 1949, *The Crucible* in 1953, and *The Diary of Anne Frank* in 1955. When Willson pitched his idea to him, he smelled a winner. Bloomgarden asked Willson to meet him in New York so they could talk about *The Music Man* in person. Once again, Willson and Rini flew across the country for what turned out to be the most unusual of all of their many auditions. Bloomgarden organized the audition at midnight in Herbert Greene's apartment—a man the Willsons had never met. As it turned out, Greene was the musical conductor for *Most Happy Fella,* and he simply could not get home any earlier. It was December 19, 1956.

A determined Willson and Rini went through the entire show, the former seated at the piano and the latter standing beside him, singing with the enthusiasm of a performer on opening night. It was the same routine they had given the agents on that dreadful night a few months past, for Siegel and his wife, and for so many others. They felt good about their performance—but then they almost always felt good about their auditions. The exhausted couple dragged themselves back to their hotel room at 4:00 a.m. and collapsed into a deep sleep. Five hours later Bloomgarden called. "Meet me at my office," he demanded. The Willsons had no idea what to expect, having encountered disappointment and heartbreak on so many occasions. So with some trepidation—and no little excitement—they prepared for the early morning invitation. Within a short time they were standing in Bloomgarden's office listening to the words they had been waiting five long years to hear: Bloomgarden and Greene loved the audition, and were going to produce *The Music Man.*

Bloomgarden admitted that when Willson first called him to talk about his new musical, he didn't recognize the caller's name. "I said to myself, 'Who the hell is Meredith Willson?' It had been so long since I heard him on the radio, I'd forgotten all about him. But he played the show through for me . . . and we signed the contract."

Signing the contract, however, was just the beginning of a long and remarkable journey. There was still a substantial amount of rewriting to be done, and now there was the matter of the cast. Who would play the lead? Several actors were discussed. Danny Kaye was the top choice, but other names were tossed around—Gene Kelly, Dan Dailey, Ray Bolger, Bert Parks, Art Carney, Jason Robards. Even slapstick comedian Milton Berle and the bombastic Jackie Gleason, the rotund comedian starring in his own hit television show, were considered for the part of Harold Hill. There was also another important matter to resolve. Who was going to direct the show?

Willson and Rini flew back to Los Angeles for Christmas. Two weeks later, Bloomgarden called them back to New York to audition in front of Moss Hart, a highly successful Broadway director. Once again, they went through the paces but Hart respectfully declined. Too corny, he said. Flying back and forth between New York and California was beginning to wear on the Willsons, so they decided to get an apartment in New York City, at least for the duration of their work on *The Music Man*.

Bloomgarden arranged yet another audition, this one for director Morton DaCosta at Bloomgarden's apartment in February of 1957. Willson didn't know DaCosta and was not formally introduced to him before the audition began. He played and Rini sang, without knowing who, among all of the people gathered in Bloomgarden's apartment, they were supposed to impress. After the performance ended, the pair were introduced to a sandy-haired man who had been standing close to the piano. Morton DaCosta liked what he heard. He agreed to direct the play, but told Willson the spastic kid had to go. It was the same advice Feuer and Martin had told him five years ago.

Willson rewrote the script again, eliminating the boy in the wheelchair. Now, however, he had to develop a character who could draw the sympathy of the audience without stealing the show. Willson had clung to his idea of showcasing the boy in the wheelchair because of his fervent belief that physically handicapped people are not automatically mentally handicapped, and he wanted the opportunity to demonstrate this to a large audience. But so many professionals could not be wrong, and now the show's director wanted a change. Willson finally agreed and scrapped the role of the crippled child. Winthrop, the little redheaded boy with the lisp, was born in his place. Winthrop was patterned after Charlie Haverdegraine, a kid Willson knew in his boyhood in Mason City. Haverdegraine had mastered one of the few musical instruments that gave young Meredith trouble—the harmonica—and for a long time Willson believed the lisp helped his young friend play the instrument.

Bloomgarden, meanwhile, spent much of his time looking for financial backers while arranging for the play to open on December 19, 1957, at the Majestic Theatre on Broadway. After five years of waiting for something to happen, things were now moving forward at a fast clip.

Casting now began in earnest. In June, the Buffalo Bills were signed as the first barbershop quartet ever to be in a Broadway show. The days were filled with auditions for the play's other roles, including actors, actresses, singers, and dancers. Work also began on costumes and set design.

There was still the matter of who would play the lead role of Harold Hill. Endless meetings and discussions were held on the subject. Bloomgarden argued that he did not have to be a song-and-dance man. An actor with a good voice could handle it. Lloyd Bridges, Van Heflin, Robert Preston, Laurence Olivier, Alec Guinness, James Whitmore, James Cagney and Andy Griffith were all were discussed. Other names from past

Robert Preston in what would eventually become
his most famous role: the lovable con man Harold
Hill. *MCPLA*

discussions also came up again, like Kaye, Bolger, Carney, Robards, and
Dailey.

Willson flew back to California to pitch the project to Kaye one more
time, and also talk with Dailey, Gene Kelly, and Phil Harris. Willson's effort
with Kaye fizzled out quickly, and he was never able to speak with him
directly. Her husband, Kaye's wife informed Willson, was not interested in
the part. The same was true for both Phil Harris and Gene Kelly; neither
had any desire to play a con man in a musical. Dailey's people were at least

interested enough to arrange for him to hear the show—which meant yet another audition for Meredith and Rini—but Dailey never showed up. The excuse given was that he had missed his flight.

The months were passing quickly and Willson and Bloomgarden still had not found their Harold Hill. In late summer, Bloomgarden arrived at Willson's Los Angeles home with Robert Preston, a veteran of stage and screen whose professional career dated back to 1938. As a child in Los Angeles, Preston had played several musical instruments and was interested in theater in high school. While attending classes at Pasadena Community Playhouse, a Paramount scout spotted him and signed the young actor to a movie contract. Prior to World War II, Preston appeared in several movies directed by Cecil B. DeMille. After service in the Army Air Corps in England, he returned home and landed roles in a number of Broadway shows. And it was on Broadway that Bloomgarden first saw Preston sing and dance. Now, after several leading men had turned down the part, Bloomgarden remembered Preston and his impressive stage presence. The actor-singer was interested in the offer, but there was a test he had to first pass. When Preston was done performing "Trouble" for Bloomgarden and Willson in Willson's living room, both men leaned back and smiled: they had found Professor Harold Hill.

The leading role opposite Harold Hill, Marian the Librarian, went to veteran stage actress and singer Barbara Cook. The Australian-born Cook hit New York as a young actress and singer in 1950. She already had a great Broadway track record, playing Ado Annie in *Oklahoma!* and Carrie in *Carousel.*

One of the toughest roles to fill was Winthrop, the recently-created boy with the lisp. Eddie Hodges, a 10-year-old, landed the part not by going through strenuous auditions, but by appearing as a contestant one night on the television game show *Name That Tune.* Rini saw him on the show while watching TV and alerted her husband and others that the youngster would be perfect as Winthrop. They watched him on the show the next week, agreed with Rini, and signed him up.

The Music Man was shaping up as Willson was pruning it down. Of the 40 songs he had written for it over the years, 22 were cut along the way. Some of the songs that made it were still being composed as rehearsals began on October 9, 1957. As a special treat for the cast, Da Costa had Willson and Rini do one more "audition," this one in front of the entire cast on the first day of rehearsals. This time they got rave reviews.

The cast and crew often worked seven days a week for the next six weeks to get the show ready for its out-of-town opening, at the Shubert Theater in Philadelphia on November 17, 1957. Broadway shows often opened in limited engagements out of town to give everyone involved a chance to work out the kinks. And there were some kinks in Philadelphia. Willson sat in the audience, taking notes on what worked and what didn't, and was rewriting dialogue and lyrics even at this point because he could see firsthand how the audience was reacting to what he had written.

Willson now clearly understood the difference between working in radio and television, and appearing in live theater. People pay good money to get in and see a performance on stage. There are no applause signs, no signs prompting the audience to laugh. They clap only if they feel like it. In Philadelphia, the sound system was so bad on opening night that it was difficult for the audience to hear some of the lyrics, and the first act ran much longer than anticipated.

Another thing that troubled Willson was that his human train—the opening number with its rhythmic lyrics and no rhymes that sounded like a train chugging along—didn't go over well at all in front of the live

Robert Preston (left), Meredith Willson (right), and Barbara Cook (Marian the Librarian) during a rehearsal for the stage version of *The Music Man*. MCPLA

audience. Many patrons sat and looked at their programs, oblivious to the fact that the show had even started. Willson, Bloomgarden, and Da Costa all knew there was work to be done before this show was ready for Broadway.

The next day, Willson had an electrician look at the sound system. He discovered that three of four speakers in the theater were faulty, and fixed them by curtain time. That night, after watching the opening number fall flat on its face for a second straight show, Willson fretted about it while casually talking to someone from the audience during intermission. The patron told him the orchestra music was too loud, and drowned out the singing. People in the audience thought they were listening to an overture before the start of the play. That's why they hadn't looked up. On the third night in Philadelphia the orchestra fell silent as the men chugged-chugged-chugged onto the stage—and the audience loved it!

From the time of the first rehearsals, Da Costa, whose nickname was "Tek," established a terrific working rapport with the cast. "I adored working with him," said Cook, who would work with him again in future musicals. "The thing that was so good about Tek is that he knew when to help and when to leave you alone. If he did encroach on your territory, you felt perfectly free to say 'leave me alone and let me struggle with it.' He didn't impose a lot of stuff on me. We hit it off perfectly."

Things were proceeding smoothly when disaster struck during a Saturday matinee about a week before the show was due to close in Philadelphia: Preston's strained vocal chords gave out in the middle of the second act. He fought his way through it—the show, after all, must go on—but everyone realized there was no way he would be able to go on Saturday night. Worse still, the Broadway opening was just a little more than a week away. Understudy Larry Douglas was pressed into service Saturday night and again on Sunday. Preston stayed in bed for two days and was back on stage Monday night, ready for his last week in Philadelphia - with a throat spray handy in his dressing room. The Pennsylvania press gave *The Music Man* decent reviews, but Philadelphia was, well, Philadelphia. Everyone—Bloomgarden, Da Costa, Willson, Preston, the rest of the cast and the entire crew—knew everything they had accomplished to that point was simply prologue for New York. Broadway was the big ticket in The Big Apple.

The tradition in New York was for a playwright to introduce his upcoming play by writing a piece for the Sunday paper prior to opening night. Willson's now-famous essay, entitled "Iowa Stubborn," appeared in the *New York Herald Tribune* on December 15, 1957:

I lived in Mason City, Iowa, till I was 16. With my folks. My brother is a very famous man in the industrial field. Light aggregate concrete. In fact, he's an expert. I don't mind telling that to you but it's the first time I've ever told it to him. That's what we call Iowa-stubborn.

My wife and I made a homecoming appearance at a home show in Des Moines seven or eight years ago and didn't receive enough applause to get us out onto the platform.

There were lots of Mason City people there, too, including several of my kissing relatives. That's what we call Iowa-contrary. ('Who do they think they are, anyway?')

In 1949, Frank Loesser said, `I think you ought to write a musical comedy about Iowa.' I thought it was a good idea and I wanted very much to do it, but I refused just to prove Frank was wrong. Goodman Ace made the same suggestion a year later and I refused again for the same reason. Nobody brought it up again for some time and I began to think they thought I couldn't do it. So, of course, I had to give it a try. That's what we call Iowa arrogance.

The existence of *The Music Man* proves Somerset Maugham's contention that anybody with a good memory can write down a story. I remember my childhood so well that each character in the show is not one but a composite of three or four different people. One possible exception could be Marian Paroo (the leading lady, played by Barbara Cook) who I think is mostly my mother, although I didn't realize this myself until the second week in Philadelphia.

Harold Hill (the starring role, played by Robert Preston) is so many people that I remember different ones every time I see the show. The period is 1912 when I was 10 years old, so I suppose some of the points of view are reflected in the 10-year-old role of Winthrop, played by Eddie Hodges. I'm pretty sure Mason City never had a mayor like David Burns' Mayor Shinn, but the lady who used to help Mama clean house on Saturdays, a wonderful German lady named Mrs. Buehler, is close to identical to Pert Kelton's Mrs. Paroo, except that the German has become Irish.

Some Iowans who have seen *The Music Man* in rehearsal have called it an Iowan's attempt to pay tribute to his home state. I'm glad they feel that way because that's what I meant it to be even though I didn't rose-color up our stubborn ways. Anyway, the show ('what there is of it, and there's a lot of it, such as it is'—sample comment from cousin Phil) has been taken off of the paper and put onto the stage with faithfulness. In taking pains and care in this regard is Morton Da Costa's best, and although I haven't been on Broadway before, I've been around Broadway long enough to observe that Morton Da Costa's best is the best there is. The same goes for Kermit Bloomgarden and Herb Greene. And the company. And there goes my last alibi."

On December 19, 1957, with Preston fully recovered from his throat problems, all the microphones and sound system equipment working in the Majestic Theatre, a new song and several dialogue changes made as late as the last week in Philadelphia—and with the orchestra silenced for the opening number—*The Music Man* opened on Broadway.

It was exactly one year to the day that Willson and Rini had auditioned the play at midnight in a stranger's New York apartment.

Actor Robert Preston dressed to the hilt as Harold Hill. After Meredith saw him in action, he proclaimed that Preston was born to play the role. Few would disagree with that assessment. *MCPLA.*

Chapter 10

"*The Music Man* is a new masterpiece . . . so rich, so funny, so
expertly done. It has more than rip-roaring entertainment.
It has strength, a strength drawn from the fertile breast
of this continent's Middle West."

— Frank Aston, *New York World-Telegram*

Jiggles and Jumps

*W*hile *The Music Man* was making a splash on Broadway,
the rest of the world was experiencing growing pains in
1957-1958, as well as some of the aches and anguishes that
had been passed on from one generation to another.

Dwight D. Eisenhower began his second term as President of the
United States on January 20. Nine months later on September 24, he
ordered federal troops into Arkansas to thwart Gov. Orville Faubus'
attempts to stop black children from enrolling at Little Rock's Central
High School. On October 4, the first man-made satellite, the Soviet
Union's *Sputnik*, was launched into space. The event triggered a decade's-
long "space race" between the world's two super powers, as each worked to
outdo the other in space and military technology. Before the end of the
year, the first large nuclear power plant in the world started up in
Shippingport, Pennsylvania, forever changing the dynamics of energy
production in the world and challenging man's uses of it. Other issues of
lesser importance were also in the news: the first international association
of bodyguards was established in Paris in December, *Bridge on the River*

Kwai won the Academy Award as best motion picture of the year, and Bobby Helms' "My Special Angel" was the hottest record on the pop charts.

Westerns were beginning to replace quiz shows as the top television programs. Tops on TV in 1957 were *Gunsmoke, The Danny Thomas Show, Tales of Wells Fargo, Have Gun, Will Travel, I've Got a Secret, The Life and Legend of Wyatt Earp, General Electric Theater* (hosted by Ronald Reagan), *The Restless Gun, December Bride,* and *You Bet Your Life,* the show hosted by Groucho Marx. One of the quiz shows that was not in the Top Ten was *The Big Surprise,* the same show Willson had unsuccessfully auditioned for in 1951 as host. His failure resulted in his return home to work on his play. And now, as 1957 drew to a close, Willson's first musical was the hottest ticket on Broadway.

"The most important thing to be said about *The Music Man,* which opened at the Majestic Theatre last night, is that it is a whopping hit," waxed John McClain in the *New York Journal-American.* "It is a new musical in the old manner: it has blare and brass. It jiggles and jumps. It has speed and style and its people are beguiling. This salute by Meredith Willson to his native Iowa will make even Oklahoma look to its laurels."

McClain was not alone in his assessment. According to John Chapman of the *New York Daily News,* "*The Music Man,* which offered itself to the season's happiest audience last evening at the Majestic Theatre, is one of the few great musical comedies of the last 26 years."

Frank Aston, writing for the *New York World-Telegram,* called the play "a new masterpiece that you'll take to your heart because it's so rich, so funny, so expertly done. It has more than rip-roaring entertainment. It has strength, a strength drawn from the fertile breast of this continent's Middle West."

Walter Kerr, concurrently perhaps the most feared and respected critic of his day, loved the show's unique opening: "Meredith Willson, librettist, composer and lyricist of the delightful new show at the Majestic has whipped out an entire first choral scene without a note of music," he noted in the *New York Herald-Tribune.* "The words, the hands, the knees and the insane Rock Island roadbed do all the work: grunts, roars, gossip, and a form of St. Vidus dance all merge into a syncopated conversation that is irresistible." This acknowledgment was quite a victory for Willson, who was absolutely delighted that Kerr had picked up on what he was trying to do: create a rhythm-without-rhyme opening that worked. He had written it in California, tinkered with it for years, fixed it in Philadelphia, and bowled over the critics with it in New York.

Brooks Atkinson in the *New York Times* told his readers: "Dollars to doughnuts, Meredith Willson dotes on brass bands. In *The Music Man,* which opened last evening at the Majestic, he has translated the thump and razzle-dazzle of brass-band lore into a warm and genial cartoon of American life. . . . If Mark Twain could have collaborated with Vachel Lindsay, they might have devised a rhythmic lark like *The Music Man* which is as American as apple pie and a Fourth of July oration."

The news and information periodicals also jumped on the band—or in this case, the Wells Fargo—wagon: *Time* magazine said the play had "unrationed, old-fashioned, bring-the-whole-family high spirits." But, the magazine cautioned: "In theme, *The Music Man* is just one more sentimental-satiric yarn about a fake who floods a dull hole with genuine gaiety. It has, besides, its sinking spells of wit and mild attacks of cuteness. More damagingly, the second act has an air of playing back much of the first, repeating all manner of effects. Fortunately, *The Music Man* can even walk backward and downhill with considerable elan; there is no denying the bounce of the show. . . . *The Music Man* is not pure cream, only nice, fresh half-and-half."

Look magazine noted proudly, "Robert Preston is America's answer to Rex Harrison," referring to the British star of the classic musical *My Fair Lady*. Syndicated columnist Walter Winchell reported an anecdote he heard from Preston: A woman who saw the musical told him, "It's the only show on Broadway to which you can take a nun with no fear of embarrassment."

Willson's sister Dixie, now 67 years old and an accomplished playwright herself, also gave her brother a good review. Four months after opening night, she wrote a glowing tribute to Willson for the *American Weekly* magazine. "Meredith," she explained, "has never told me the number of times he rewrote *The Music Man* between 1951 when he began it, and late 1957 when it premiered. But I do know that he wrote 38 songs for it which was whittled down to 17. His friend Franklin Lacey helped him with the storyline. . . . They say Meredith will make between three and four million dollars. I doubt if making a million matters a great deal to him, but I rise to echo the comment of Editor Earl Hall, who said in the Mason City *Globe-Gazette's* proud account of the New York opening: "It couldn't happen to a nicer man."

In a letter to a friend, however, Dixie claimed something altogether different. In fact, she boldly asserted that the original idea for *The Music Man* was hers, and that she had envisioned Meredith as playing the lead. According to Dixie, she had discussed the idea with Meredith and that the two had agreed to collaborate on it. She even claimed to have made the first contacts with producers Feuer and Martin. The project was put on hold, contended Dixie, only because of the deaths of her literary agent, Jacob Milk, and Murray Anderson, another close friend, which had put her in a state of deep distress. Meredith, she explained, followed through with the show on his own and got Bloomgarden to produce it and Preston to star in it.

In her letter, Dixie complained that her brother's method of producing a play was exactly the opposite of how she thought shows should be packaged:

> No Fifth Avenue tailor would consent to work by the method of making a suit, then taking it up and down the Avenue looking for someone whom it would fit. . . . When I first came from Iowa (via Greenwich Village Follies chorus), I had already proven myself to be a born playwright with smash after smash in the Midwest, astonishing Chicago producers who were by no means less than professional.
>
> I was, in turn, astonished to discover the stupid New York approach to getting a play up in lights. Even 'green' as I was in matters of Broadway protocol, I made up my mind that I would write plays by my own formula or not at all. i.e. I would contact a 'right' star . . . as the first step . . . not the last. Together we would discuss the basic pattern of the play to be created until it thrilled and satisfied both of us or proved that it wasn't good enough. In other words, we would pick our material, style and measurements before cutting the suit. When and if the results were sufficiently thrilling and inspiring to the star, we would seek the next necessary approval, that of the man who would pay for it, the producer. . . .
>
> Thus covering the preliminaries, we would turn out a 'suit' whose style, material, size and fit (in the case of a play, its story, timing, balance, humor and other quality values) would be complete when delivered without dependence on later ripping, altering, restyling and correcting wrinkles or sagging or shoulder pads in the wrong place.
>
> By the usual method, a play is written, then given to an agent for peddling until it is old hat and lost in the discard. Or, if accepted, producer and director require the inevitable changes, but by this time, have exhausted the kicks until they don't know whether it has any more or not.
>
> All their hashing and rehashing has lost any capacity they have for reaction to the very values which an audience must feel if the play is to be a smash. Last of all, they elect the star upon whose genius the thing will sink or swim, the last person to find out if the role makes her heart beat faster . . . or not at all.
>
> I still insist my way is the only way to create a play which can make every heart beat faster. If it hasn't been created with values which at first reading will be thrilling all the way down the line, I don't think the world has room for it in these crowded, complicated days.

Dixie's disgust with how Meredith went about getting his show on Broadway was simply a disagreement as to a matter of style. Her contention that she deserved credit for helping write *The Music Man*, however, is a far different matter. Feuer and Martin, who produced plays and movies together for 50 years and were in on *The Music Man* at the beginning, never acknowledged that Dixie deserved credit. And Meredith was never averse to sharing credit. Franklin Lacey, the man he met in San Diego who agreed to help him, for example, is credited with being co-author of *The Music Man* book.

In 1962, when Dixie was 72 years old, she took the time to type an angry and rather sad 19-page typewritten letter to *Globe-Gazette* editor Earl Hall. The missive was one long plea for the credit she thought she deserved. According to Dixie, it was she who "conceived in foundation and scenes of the work that became *The Music Man*, this success had been accomplished and sold before Meredith finished and scored it."

Hall, who knew Willson well and had seen the early drafts of *The Music Man* while visiting Meredith in California, as well as the finished version on Broadway, was firm in his frosty reply and unyielding in his support of Meredith:

> Dear Dixie,
>
> Your extended letter, with preface and picture, has been received and carefully read.
>
> In candor, I must tell you I am in total disagreement with you in regard to your appraisal of Meredith's character, as distinguished from his talents . . . .
>
> *The Music Man*, as it revealed itself that opening night on Broadway (Dec. 19, 1957) and the play I had seen presented in admittedly sketchy manner in Brentwood, had no relationship except for the retention of some of Meredith's tunes.
>
> Even with the revolutionary change of story in the finished form, Dixie, it would fall flat on its face were it not for Meredith's music.
>
> You are carrying a torch for a "Music Man" that never got off the ground.

Willson's hometown paper was quick to publish every positive review it could find. Those that were less than complimentary were treated with disdain. "I have spotted only two adverse estimations of Meredith Willson's *The Music Man* since it opened, wrote columnist Enoch Norem. "Both, significantly enough, were from keyhole gossip columnists. One of these critics was Dorothy Kilgallen, whose field of operations is New York; the other is Sheila Graham, whose beat is Hollywood. Neither has ever been referred to as a 'kindly philosopher.' It isn't surprising that a production wholly free from smut and ugliness would lack appeal for gals who specialize on items from the gutter," he wrote.

The Music Man ran on Broadway for 1,375 performances—almost four years. It won eight Tony Awards in 1958, including Best Musical and Best Performance by an Actor (Preston). It was also awarded the recording industry's first Grammy Award for its outstanding music. The Majestic Theater grossed $70,909 a week for the entire run of the show. Willson received a seven percent royalty, which provided him with what he called "take-home pay" of $4,963.63 a week. Feuer and Martin, the show's original producers, would have become rich had they stayed with the project, but they were already highly successful when *The Music Man* came their way and continued their successful careers long afterward. Together, they produced a dozen Broadway shows and The Tony Awards television program. Feuer also produced the movies *Cabaret* and *A Chorus Line*. Neither Feuer nor Martin missed a meal, but they did miss a big payday by passing up on *The Music Man*.

CBS, too, lost a big opportunity when its officials walked out of the audition before it had ended. The station's officials, who had called the show "too corny," had been offered the opportunity to finance it for $300,000. In return, CBS would have received 40 percent of the profits, plus exclusive recording and television rights.

In January of 1958, a month after the show opened, Willson was asked by the *New York Times* how he survived while he struggled so long to get *The Music Man* completed. He answered, as he had in the past, with the eight words that had sustained him in more ways than one: "May the Good Lord Bless and Keep You."

The phenomenal success generated by *The Music Man's* Broadway run bred triumph in different arenas. By March 1958, five record albums with songs from *The Music Man* had been produced, with the original cast album, released by Capitol Records, rising to the country's number one seller. In addition, three major movie studios—Warner Brothers, 20th Century Fox, and Metro Goldwyn Mayer—were negotiating for film rights. Willson was well on his way to making the kind of money his sister had predicted he would.

On July 21, 1958, *The Music Man* was the big story of *Time* magazine, with Willson, Preston, and Barbara Cook pictured proudly on the weekly's cover. Willson showed his gratitude in a letter to the editor published the following week. The missive consisted of just four words: "My cup runneth over."

The Iowa native's sudden rise to real fame after decades of ceaseless effort also gave him a platform from which to pontificate, particularly about the state of music in the late 1950s. One reporter, for example, asked him his opinion of the latest teen-age craze—something called "rock and roll." Willson was not impressed with the new genre.

"The people of this country do not have any conception of the evil being done by rock and roll," Willson responded. "It is a plague as far reaching as any plague we have ever had and now it's become international in scope. My preoccupation with this creeping paralysis is not with the lascivious quality, the suggestive dancing that goes with it. This is bad and it's been condemned before. My complaint," he continued, "is that it just isn't music. It's utter garbage and it should not be confused in any way with anything related with music or verse."

He appreciated that some might misconstrue his harsh and puritanical view of rock and roll. "It's very difficult to say these things without sounding like a preacher. I'll also be accused of sour grapes because it's true, I have another kind of music to sell. But in rock and roll, we're talking about a guy who can only play two chords, who has no craftsmanship, no natural ability, who is not a musician in any sense of the word."

Willson's scathing critique of music's new "plague" was tempered by his good old fashioned Iowa folksiness, a demeanor that came to him naturally. He enjoyed his many opportunities to charm his admiring press with it. One interviewer was told of how he loved to take a walk, and tried to do it every morning at 10:15 in Los Angeles. In New York, he took a daily walk between 2: 00 and 4:00 p.m. He said the difference between walking in Los Angeles and walking in New York was that in New York, you had to have a destination. You didn't just walk for the sake of walking. "I work when I walk," he said. "My mind talks turkey during that afternoon walk. I don't trust a lyric until I've gone over it and over it. There comes a point when you're finally done. When you know you know."

Willson said that often in New York, he would walk from his apartment on 88th Street to Frank Loesser's apartment on 35th Street, and that he would frequently stop and talk to a friend, Joe Dine, whose office was somewhere in between. On one of these walks, while *The Music Man* was still being written, he said he "thought up" the song "Lida Rose," which became one of the popular numbers in the second act. He didn't run into Joe Dine that day. If he had, he explained, "Lida Rose" might never have been written.

A man from Los Angeles named George Thomas had seen the show and loved it. He penned a long and fascinating letter to his cousin, Robert Brooke, an attorney in West Liberty, Iowa. "Do you remember the last time you were here and we went on a set at Paramount Studios and I introduced you to a handsome young actor named Robert Preston and he sat down and had a nice long visit with us?" asked Thomas. "Well, he hammered along as a pretty fair country dramatic actor, never getting too high in the dough but doing pretty good. He was never in a musical picture in his life, and all of a sudden he bounces up in a Broadway musical that is such a smash hit, it will probably top *My Fair Lady*."

The lead role Preston landed was in a play, continued Thomas' letter, "written, lock, stock and barrel, story, book, lyrics and music by an old Mason City, Iowa boy named Meredith Willson and is called *The Music Man* and Preston sings and dances like crazy and is now the toast of Broadway. Willson played piccolo with Sousa and the New York Philharmonic and then came to California and got in radio, conducting and composing. He wrote a novel and two semi-autobiographies of his Iowa boyhood, one called *And There I Stood With My Piccolo* and the other I've forgotten the title. They are probably both in your library and you might want to read them sometime."

Thomas then proceeded to share with his Iowa cousin an amazing Willson anecdote:

> Anyway, I know this Willson feller and know a wonderful thing that happened to him. When our Bobbie was first married, he lived in Westwood, near the UCLA campus, and right across Willshire from him was a little shack in the grove of trees, back off the street, where a struggling congregation was trying to establish a church. They finally made it and built a modest building right on the boulevard. We watched it go up from Bobbie's windows.
>
> Anyhoo, one morning, Meredith Willson and his part-Russian wife were driving along Willshire and saw a few stragglers going into this little church. On a sudden impulse, he turned to his wife and said, 'let's go in. It looks like such a friendly place.' He stopped his car, parked and they went in.
>
> The pastor had chosen as his sermon, 'People I Would Like to Meet.' In the midst of his sermon he stopped, picked up a book and began to read. It was a bit of homely Iowa philosophy, and of course to the amazement of Willson and his wife, they realized he was reading from Willson's own autobiography. Tears streamed down both their cheeks. When the pastor finished reading, he stopped for a moment and said, 'Now there is a man I would like to meet—a man who can write, so simply and so eloquently, of the little precious things of life'—or words to that effect.
>
> Well, the Willsons didn't hear much of the rest of the sermon. Meredith kind of slunk down in his seat and tried to hide, although he was sure no one in the church knew him by sight. He had done little TV, only radio. When church was out, the pastor took his stand at the door and shook hands with everyone. The last out were the Willsons.

Meredith offered his hand. 'I'm Meredith Willson,' he said. The pastor liked to drop dead right there.

According to Thomas, "The Willsons went back the next Sunday, eventually joined the church and that little congregation now has one of the finest, best drilled choirs in LA, picked and drilled of course by Meredith, who has also composed some music for their group singing." Thomas finished his letter to his West Liberty cousin with this bit of advice: "If you get a chance to hear the music from *The Music Man*, do so."

Meanwhile, halfway across the country, the folks in Mason City were ecstatic about the hometown boy's play and his success. Many planned vacation trips to New York to see the show. Evelyn Walls and her two daughters, Madelyn and Esther, attended in the summer of 1958. Their seats were in the Majesic Theater's third balcony. As they waited for the opening curtain, Mrs. Walls became dizzy from being up so high. Her daughters summoned help and asked if they could exchange their tickets for seats in an area of the theater closer to ground level. When a theater official discovered they were from Mason City, Iowa, he pulled some strings and got them seats in the fifth row of the front section.

"I didn't dare tell him that I was the town librarian," Madelyn Walls said afterwards. "He would have thought we were a real con outfit for sure."

Candid Camera Scenes of the Rehearsals

Peter Gennaro puts Tammy Grimes
through her paces for one of the
dance numbers.

THE
UNSINKABLE
MOLLY BROWN

Tammy Grimes and Harve Presnell

Tammy Grimes and Mitchell Gregg

"A
smash
hit"
JOHN
MCCLAIN
Journal-
American

Harve Presnell, Tammy Grimes, Edith Meiser,
Jack Harrold and Cameron Prud'Homme
in a hilarious moment.

Photos from the play *The Unsinkable Molly Brown. MCPLA*

Chapter 11

"All you have to do to fill a theater with warmth and cheer, bounce
and excitement, is to do an old-fashioned musical comedy, [and]
hire Meredith Willson to write the music and key lyrics steeped
deep in the Americana in which he excels."

— Whitney Bolton, *New York Morning Telegraph*

The Unsinkable Molly Brown

n August 18, 1958, *The Music Man* began performances on
both coasts. While Robert Preston was still impressing
audiences on Broadway as Professor Harold Hill, Forrest
Tucker took up the role in the national road company. The musical
opened at the Philharmonic Auditorium in Los Angeles with some subtle
changes to appeal to a west coast audience. The barber shoppers were the
"Buffalo Bills" in New York, but called the "Frisco Four" in California. A
change that delighted the home folks in Mason City was the successful
audition of Lynn Potter of Mason City, who won the part of Winthrop
Paroo.

The huge success of *The Music Man* made Willson not only a rich
man, but a highly sought-after composer. He had struggled for five years to

complete his first musical and had to audition it in a stranger's apartment at midnight to get it on Broadway. Now he was flooded with offers.

Meredith and Rini, meanwhile, had developed a routine they performed in concerts all over the country called "*And Then I Wrote The Music Man.*" Willson would open by playing a few bars of "Seventy-Six Trombones" on the piano while starting to tell the story of Harold Hill—"Professor Harold Hill, if you please." As Willson told the story, he would hit chords on the piano to emphasize his points. He told of Professor Hill coming to River City in 1912 to sell band instruments to the kids—(chord!), and uniforms (chord!), and instruction books (chord!), and lessons (chord!).

Willson told the story all the way through, pausing only for him, Rini, or both of them to sing the songs. At one point, he instructed Rini to go "ch, ch ch" at certain points in the "Trouble in River City" number so he could catch his breath. The concerts were fun and they helped promote the show.

While negotiations were under way to make the Broadway musical into a motion picture, Willson's expertise was being courted for other Broadway productions. He signed on to do the music for *The Unsinkable Molly Brown*, a play based on a book written by Richard Morris and scheduled to be directed by Dore Schary. "I saw in it the kinds of things I believe fit my kind of interest—period Americana and the love story of two characters I could like," he told the *New York Times*. "I said 'if you'll take the cussin' out of there and be mindful of beautifying the love story, I'm your boy.'"

In Dore Schary, Willson worked with one of the most dynamic directors of stage and screen. The outspoken liberal thumbed his nose at U.S. Senator Joseph McCarthy when he attempted to blacklist the director for his liberal causes. Schary was at one time national chairman of the B'nai Brith's Anti-Defamation League, and had served as commissioner of cultural affairs for the city of New York. He won an Academy Award in 1938 for his screenplay of *Boys Town*, and served as chief of production for Metro Goldwyn Mayer studios from 1948 to 1956. After he was fired by MGM, Schary moved to New York and began producing plays for Broadway. One of these he wrote and produced was *Sunrise at Campobello*, the story of Franklin and Eleanor Roosevelt.

The Unsinkable Molly Brown was not as light-hearted as *The Music Man.* Instead of a con artist trying to hoodwink a small town, the show dealt with the story of an illiterate woman at the turn of the century married to a prospector who discovers $19 million in gold. Molly, one of the survivors of the sinking of *Titanic*—hence, the "unsinkable" label—tells her life story to

Dore Schary, one of the country's finest directors, together with Rini and Meredith Willson on the set of *The Unsinkable Molly Brown*. MCPLA

the other lucky souls gathered about her in a lifeboat to keep their spirits up. The Broadway show starred Tammy Grimes in the title role, with Harve Presnell by her side as leading man.

Grimes, a veteran actress and comedienne who had many stage performances to her credit, had never landed a starring role until *Molly Brown*. She later claimed she got the role after singing "Melancholy Baby" at her audition. Her wit, grit, and tireless efforts proved an inspiration to the entire cast. Though her name was billed below the title, making her a supporting actress, she obviously had the lead role, and her outstanding performance earned her a Tony award for best actress in a musical comedy.

Rehearsals for *Molly Brown* began on the morning of August 29, 1960, at the Ambassador Theater in New York. Schary assembled the entire company on stage, including the stage hands, and had them stand in a semi-circle around him. He began the first rehearsal with a full reading of the entire play so everyone could begin their work by seeing the show as a whole and how they fit in. Tammy Grimes sat in a chair at stage right. When it was time for her to perform, she jumped out of her chair, bounded over to the piano at stage left and belted out her song. Her enthusiasm energized the entire cast on the very first day.

For his part, Willson at one point jumped in and sang an impromptu duet with Grimes to give her an idea of the tempo he wanted in a particular song. The following day, groups of cast members went their separate ways: dancers to the Belasco Theater stage and singers to special studios; the actors and actresses remained at the Ambassador. After running for about two weeks at the Schubert Theatre in Philadelphia—just as *The Music Man* had, so cast, crew, producer, director, conductor and composer could work out the imperfections—the show opened on Broadway on November 3, 1960.

Earl Hall, editor of the hometown *Globe-Gazette*, visited Willson in Philadelphia and attended one of the early performances there. "Except for what I saw and heard that night," he told his readers, "I'd never sense how vastly important to the success of a theater production is this period of experimentation and revision in some city other than New York." An hour and a half before curtain time, the orchestra, under the direction of Herb Greene, one of Willson's trusted cohorts with *The Music Man*, rehearsed

Endless rehearsals. Author Richard Morris (left), Tammy Grimes (center), and Meredith Willson (right), preparing for the stage version of *The Unsinkable Molly Brown*. MCPLA

revisions in the score while a nervous Meredith Willson paced back and forth talking to various musicians about what he was trying to achieve with the music. While all of this was going on, dancers in leotards pranced through parts of their routines, concentrating so much on their work that they were oblivious to what was going on around them.

The curtain went up, the show opened—and disaster struck. Tammy Grimes—"Molly"—lost her voice, just like Robert Preston three years earlier when *The Music Man* opened in Philadelphia. She missed the next six performances. The critics were kind, but cautious. *Variety* informed its readers that the show "had a superior score by Meredith Willson, an unexpectedly forceful, often off-beat book by Richard Morris, gorgeous scenic backgrounds and a vibrant performance by Tammy Grimes, a bright prospect for Broadway." But, *Variety* warned, "it is not a show that can be taken for granted. Plenty of work needs to be done in sharpening, cutting and rearranging."

Willson wasn't bothered by the mixed early reviews. In fact, he found them helpful. "For the most part, the critics have been right," he said. "Their suggestions have been helpful to us in getting the show ready for New York, where we know the reviewers will be even more critical."

After the opening night in Philadelphia, many in the cast and crew went for sandwiches and a "post mortem" at Lew Tendler's, a popular restaurant owned by a former lightweight boxing champion. Tammy Grimes sulked about her performance and questioned some of the changes that Schary was thinking about making. Other performances were criticized—someone mouthed their lines without feeling, someone else didn't come down stage at the right time. Leading man Harve Presnell seemed to have "lockjaw" every time he was in a romantic scene with Grimes.

One of the other patrons in the restaurant had seen the show earlier that evening. Seated nearby, he listened to the performers' dejected evaluations of the performance. "You are being too hard on yourselves," was his gentle admonishment.

"If you think we're tough, you should see what those New York critics will do to us," Willson told the observer, laughing as he said it.

The show opened at the Winter Garden on November 3, 1960, right across the street from where *The Music Man* was going strong and, in another month, would begin its fourth year.

Major changes were made in "Molly" after the mixed Philadelphia performances. A prologue at the start of the show was cut. The scene with Molly taking control of the lifeboat was lengthened and strengthened. All in all, the show was tightened up considerably. If spontaneous clapping was any indication, the audience in New York seemed to enjoy it more than the audience in Philadelphia.

Frank Aston, writing for the *New York World-Telegram*, loved it. "*The Unsinkable Molly Brown*," he wrote, "is delectable at the start, middle and finish. Meredith Willson wrote its music and lyrics. Comedy is lusty—yowling miners, 'royal guests' with mock processional with crowns, and Miss Grimes with her croaks, chin angle, shoulder pushing, sturdy legs, funny tummy line, cuss words and general adorability."

Critic Walter Kerr in the *New York Herald-Tribune* liked it as well. "Tammy Grimes mesmerized me at the Winter Garden. . . . Meredith Willson's music keeps the timpani popping." In the *New York Morning Telegraph*, Whitey Bolton told his readers, "All you have to do to fill a theater with warmth and cheer, bounce and excitement, is to do an old-fashioned musical comedy, hire Meredith Willson to write the music and key lyrics steeped deep in the Americana in which he excels, and, if the principal role fits, have Tammy Grimes explode all over the place."

Not every review was positive, however. *Time* magazine's critique was less than enthusiastic. "The chronicle of Molly Brown . . . is often given funny-paper treatment. The show has an altogether loose-leaf structure, while the Meredith Willson score is not up to *The Music Man's* and has nothing as infectious as 'Seventy-Six Trombones.' But it gives kind of a joyous blare to the evening." The "joyous blare" continued on Broadway for 532 performances.

When Willson struggled to get *The Music Man* on Broadway, he was a newcomer and nothing came easy, not even response from record companies to the cast album and singles from the show. With *Molly Brown*, he was an established Broadway kingpin and album sales were a natural outgrowth of the successful Broadway hit. Willson was also "a smarter and wiser man," as Professor Harold Hill would say. Willson and those representing him refused to accept any deals with record companies until the show was in its fourth week. It was a smart move. The delay allowed the show's many potential hit songs to be hyped, which in turn forced the record companies to sweeten their financial proposals for the music.

Capitol records produced the cast album, as well as an album by Guy Lombardo and Jonah Jones. Capitol also produced several singles from the show sung by Dinah Shore, Tex William, Gordon MacRae, Les Baxter, Janice Harper, Jack Marshall, Nat "King" Cole, and The Four Preps. In addition, the record company produced a "novelty" single featuring Stan Kenton, Billy May, Nelson Riddle, and Ray Anthony singing one of the show's peppiest songs, "Belly Up to the Bar, Boys."

Willson did not stay in New York long. A week after the play opened, he and Rini made a quick trip to Mason City to take part in the dedication of the Rosalie Reiniger Willson educational wing of the First Congregational Church, a project that benefitted from a $50,000 contribution from Willson.

Dixie Willson, who lived in New Jersey, sent her best wishes to the Rev. Robert Stone and the hometown congregation, thanking them for naming the addition after her mother. She said she was glad Meredith was able to be so generous in his giving. Her brother Cedric, she explained, would not be able to do much since he was paying for his children to attend college. As for her—she sent her prayers.

Ever the eccentric, Dixie arranged her own tribute to her mother through a theater chain in New Jersey. On August 24, 1962, the Walter Reade theaters presented a plaque to Dixie in recognition of her mother's work with children's productions in Mason City. It was an odd thing to do. Rosalie Willson had never been to New Jersey and had no connection with the theaters.

Dixie tried to justify the presentation in a long and rambling letter to *Globe-Gazette* editor Earl Hall. According to her, Rosalie had spent much of her life pining for public recognition for her church productions and theatrical abilities, to no avail. It was recognition she deeply deserved, argued Dixie, who also took the opportunity to level a shot against her brother Meredith for failing to appreciate or recognize their mother's talent. "I will probably bring rather than send" the plaque, explained Dixie. "I hate to take any chance of anything happening to it in shipping or delivery. I intend to try and come home within 2 or 3 weeks." The plaque arrived in Mason City shortly thereafter; Dixie never showed up.

Hall was outraged by Dixie's charges. His response, dated September 14, 1962, was sharp and to the point. "No woman in my 42 years in Mason City has been as honored in memory as your Mother, whose friendship I treasured. Nobody else known to me has her name inscribed in stone on a church edifice."

The *Globe's* editor was equally pointed in his response to Dixie's accusations that Meredith had not done enough to honor their mother. "In far fewer words but with no less sincerity," Hall retorted, "I've heard Meredith reverence the memory of his mother."

He wasn't finished. "Why weren't you here for the dedication? Why didn't you come with your poem? Why didn't you avail yourself of the opportunity to contribute to the cost of the unit?"

Meredith leads children in song in the new children's wing of the First Congregational Church in Mason City. He contributed $50,000 to the construction of the Rosalie Reiniger Willson Wing, named after his mother. Rosalie Willson was superintendent of the Sunday School of the church for more than 30 years. According to daughter Dixie, her mother lost her position when church elders deemed her too old to continue. *Mason City Globe-Gazette*

"Maybe [others] will see the need for your plaque and your story glorifying your Mother and down-grading your brother," concluded Hall. "But I want no part of it. And I would be less than honest if I didn't let you know that right now." As far as Hall was concerned, the award Dixie arranged was merely her way of offsetting what her brother had done to honor their mother (the $50,000 donation from Willson for the Rosalie Reiniger Willson wing), and had little to do with Rosalie personally.

Dixie dutifully accepted the plaque that she had convinced the theaters to create. In her acceptance speech, Dixie told the audience at the Mayfair, New Jersey, theater:

> The dream of all of her years was that she might some time, somehow span the distance from that small town (Mason City) to the world's important theaters by discovering and guiding earnest hopefuls into the areas of top bracket success. It is in recognition of her selfless service to our town that Mason City's Congregational church, where she supervised young activities for many years, built a handsome wing last year, dedicated and named the "Rosalie Reiniger Willson Chapel,"

where, as you have just heard, Mr. Harry Wiener, manager of your Walter Reade shore theaters, say this impressive plaque is to be sent and permanently placed.

Meredith's most recent score, meanwhile, continued racking up one success after another. *The Unsinkable Molly Brown* was made into a movie with Debbie Reynolds cast as the lead. It, too, was well received by critics and fans alike.

The real Molly Brown, who survived the sinking of *Titanic* in 1912, lived on for another eight decades after the tragedy. According to her, she was never called "the unsinkable Molly Brown" and had never heard the expression until the play opened on Broadway in 1960.

Debbie Reynolds sporting "the monkey shawl," one of the fashion trends spawned by the movie version of *The Unsinkable Molly Brown*. MCPLA

Meredith Willson holds up a happy child in 1968 along Mason City's Federal Avenue—the main route of the legendary North Iowa Band Festival Parade, which often brought Willson home. *MCPLA*

Chapter 12

"If I stood a little straighter and a little taller than my years might normally permit, it was chiefly because I'm from Mason City, Iowa."
— Meredith Willson, in the *Mason City Globe Gazette*

From Broadway to Hollywood to Mason City

By March of 1958, three major Hollywood studios (Warner Brothers, 20th Century Fox, and Metro Goldwyn Mayer) were negotiating for the film rights to *The Music Man*. Several independent companies were also vying for it. Frank Sinatra, Gene Kelly, Bing Crosby, and George Sidney also expressed an interest in starring in it.

Willson left the negotiating to the William Morris agency, saying only that he wanted to have the movie shot on special sets constructed in his home town of Mason City. Warner Brothers won the right to do the film, but only after agreeing to one other Willson stipulation. The studio wanted either Sinatra or Cary Grant for the lead role. "You don't get it unless Bob Preston comes with it," said Willson. Sinatra had been so certain he would get the part that when he saw Willson while negotiations were still going on, he asked, "When are we going to start shooting, Meredith?"

Academy Award winner Shirley Jones was cast as Marian the Librarian for the film version of *The Music Man*. Here, Jones and Willson take a moment on the set to discuss one of the songs. MCPLA

With Robert Preston's firm grip on Harold Hill, the producers cast about for the perfect Marian the Librarian. They found her in Shirley Jones. a beautiful and accomplished actress with a wonderful voice and powerful stage presence. In addition to being an Academy Award winner, Shirley brought one other distinction to the shooting of *The Music Man*:

she was pregnant. She wore several layers of clothing to cover it up, but every once in a while, something beyond her control would occur. In the famous footbridge scene, when the amiable scoundrel Harold Hill and the prudish Marian were about to kiss, the baby kicked—and Preston felt it.

"What the heck was that?" he exclaimed, looking down in shock.

"That's Patrick Michael Cassidy," announced his co-star. They both laughed and re-shot the scene—without interruption.

Willson didn't get his wish to have the movie shot in Mason City, but he was adamant about not leaving his hometown out of the hoopla. The grateful native arranged for a special press "premiere" at the Palace Theater in Mason City. The showing would be held in conjunction with the annual North Iowa Band Festival, the highlight of which was a parade down Federal Avenue, which ran north to south through the heart of downtown "River City." The annual parade featured dozens of high school bands and was a summer showcase for young people anxious to show what they could do with their musical instruments.

The Band Festival has a long and proud tradition in Mason City, and is one of the largest annual festivals of any kind in Iowa. Watching it gives one the feeling of stepping into a Meredith Willson production. In fact, he had nothing to do with starting it. The first Band Festival was held in 1928 in observance of Mason City's 75th anniversary. Five out-of-town high school bands joined the Mason City High School band to provide music for the celebration. Eight years later, the Iowa Bandmasters Association held its annual meeting in Mason City. It was decided another band festival should be held. The 1936 parade attracted 18 high school bands. The rousing success prompted organizers and citizens to plan a similar event for the following year. And thus the tradition was born. It is as much a part of summer in North Iowa as the smell of hay and corn that's knee-high by the Fourth of July. Its popularity grew so that by 1941, 56 high school bands from several states participated in the parade.

In 1958, with *The Music Man* setting box office records on Broadway. Willson and Rini returned to Mason City for the biggest Band Festival ever, held in their honor. The couple rode in the front of the parade and waved to the thousands of spectators that had been quietly lining the street since early morning. When the Mason City band, marching immediately behind the Willsons, began thundering out "Seventy-Six Trombones," its composer could no longer contain himself. Without any warning, he jumped out of the slow-moving car and headed straight for the drum major marching a few yards behind him. Meredith grabbed the baton from the surprised high schooler and led the band down Federal Avenue. The crowd stood and cheered, roaring its approval as its hometown hero

The cast of *The Music Man* gathers to celebrate Meredith Willson's birthday in Los Angeles just a month before the movie's premiere in Mason City, Iowa. The cake reads "Happy Birthday From The River City Folks to The Leading Citizen." (From left to right): Rini, director Morton Da Costa, Shirley Jones, and Willson. MCPLA

marched past Central Park, where the baton-wielding Willson had played as a child. Willson's spontaneous act is a memory that is a part of his legend in Mason City, and a photograph of him leading the band is one of the most well-known and revered pictures in Mason City history.

A highlight of that parade was a special "Music Man" band made up of 208 musicians from 22 high schools that included 76 trombones and 110 cornets. The rest of the parade included 30 floats, including a dozen with a "Music Man" theme and 93 high-stepping marching bands.

When Willson came back home again four years later in 1962, he not only brought the cast and the director of *The Music Man* with him, but the movie as well. The fact that a major motion picture was being premiered

Robert Preston (left), Shirley Jones (center), and Ronnie Howard as Winthrop on the movie set of *The Music Man*. MCPLA

for the press in a little Iowa farm town instead of big city was not lost on its grateful citizens. It was also a publicity bonanza for the film. The marketing possibilities for such an event were magnificent, and the Hollywood press corps flew to Mason City to see what all the excitement was about. Their stories, published in newspapers all over the country, provided *The Music Man* with a deluge of advance publicity before it opened in the big cities like New York and Los Angeles.

No one could remember so many dignitaries arriving in one plane at the Mason City Municipal Airport. When the door opened, out stepped

The stars of *The Music Man* arrive in Mason City for the gala movie premiere. Shirley Jones (front), is followed down the stairs by Morton Da Costa and Robert Preston, who seem to be enjoying a light moment.
Mason City Globe Gazette

Meredith and Rini Willson enjoy an Iowa picnic and hometown hospitality at a
dinner honoring the movie's premiere and the town's number one son. *Mason
City Globe Gazette*

Meredith and Rini Willson, Morton Da Costa, Robert Preston, Shirley
Jones, and the youngster, Ronnie Howard, who was cast as the lisping
Winthrop. All of them mingled with townspeople and rode in the parade,
marveling the whole time at the size of it—more than 100 bands
participated and the floats were more spectacular than ever. Ordinarily,
the parade units consisted of decorated vehicles promoting businesses,
fancy cars driven by residents who wanted to show them off, church groups
promoting their vacation bible schools, and occasional floats. This year was
different. Warner Brothers supplemented the Chamber of Commerce's
$35,000 festival budget by contributing $175,000. The festival was
expanded to three days instead of one, so that the stars could have a chance
to soak in some of the Iowa hospitality that Willson had been bragging
about for three decades. Seventy-five thousand people, or three times the
population of Mason City at that time, jammed the streets to catch a
glimpse of the celebrities and enjoy the grand parade.

The movie premiere was held on the evening of June 19, 1962. Arthur
Godfrey, the master of ceremonies, was the first to arrive. His distinct voice

These are some of the most popular images of Willson, taken at the height of his success. Overwhelmed by the crowd's enthusiasm, Meredith whisked the baton away from a drum majorette so he could lead the 1962 parade himself down Federal Avenue—the same street he walked as a boy. *Mason City Globe Gazette*

introduced the honored guests as they arrived, one by one, at the Palace Theater. To the dismay of many Mason City natives, few got to see the movie that night because there was no room for them. The small theater was jammed beyond capacity with Hollywood personalities, state and local officials and, of course, the press. Still, some 4,000 spectators lined the streets around the Palace to enjoy the special event.

"You don't have any idea what this means to us who live east of the Hudson or west of the San Bernadino Valley," announced Godfrey. "You don't have any idea of how much of real America you are. As we watched the thousands of youngsters march today, it brought a tear to my eye. *The Music Man* is a great show but it has no comparison to what we saw here today."

As guests appeared, Godfrey went to work. The VIPs included Iowa Governor Norman Erbe; Mason City Mayor George Menden and his wife; Vicki Ross, a high school senior from the nearby little town of Britt who that afternoon had been crowned the 1962 Band Festival queen; Morton Da Costa; the Buffalo Bill singers; Hollywood columnist Hedda Hopper; Ronnie Howard; U.S. Sens. Burke Hickenlooper and Jack Miller; Shirley Jones, Robert Preston and Meredith and Rini Willson.

The *Globe-Gazette* summed up the day's activities by reporting, "76 trombones, 76-degree weather and 76,000 persons made June 19 a day to remember for 'The Music Man.'" Willson was overwhelmed by what he called "the joyful vibrations" of Mason City's own special kind of national music festival. "If I stood a little straighter and a little taller than my years might normally permit, it was chiefly because I'm from Mason City, Iowa."

Buoyed by the Mason City publicity, *The Music Man* "premiered" in New York and Los Angeles a few weeks later, and then spread to theaters across the country. *Variety* offered one of the early reviews of the movie. "Allowing something of slowness at the very start and the necessities of the musical way of telling a story, plus the atmosphere of Iowa in 1912, that's about the only criticism of an otherwise bustling, punching, handsomely dressed and ultimately endearing super-musical and wide-screen and color. *The Music Man* is superior entertainment."

"Call this a triumph," continued *Variety*. . .

> a classic of corn, small town nostalgia and American love of a parade. Dreamed up in the first instance out of the Iowa memories of Meredith Willson, fashioned into his first legit offering with his long radio musicianship fully manifest therein, the transfer to the screen has been accomplished by Morton DaCosta as producer- director with faithful adherence to Willson's and his own original work. . . .
>
> But the only choice for the title role, Bob Preston, is the big proof of showmanship in the casting. Warner might have secured bigger

(Opposite) "His dark hair, usually neatly parted," *San Francisco Chronicle* columnist Herb Caen had once written, "becomes a waving mass as he leans from the podium and implores his musicians to 'Give! Give!'" Meredith directs an elementary school band during a visit home in 1968. MCPLA

screen names but it is impossible to imagine any of them matching Preston's authority. . . . His know-how in this film is as close to a tour-de-force as is likely to be seen in the calendar year 1962. Not only does he project verve, singing and dancing with a beguiling style of his own creation, but his acting has remarkable plausibility.

The little boy with the stammer and the bashful ways is a small gem as impersonated by Ronnie Howard. He stays safely away from precociousness in all of his scenes.

Twenty-five years later, Howard, who was part of the entourage in the Mason City premiere extravaganza, returned to northern Iowa as a famous movie director. Some scenes from his new movie were going to be shot on location at a factory in Charles City, Iowa, about 30 miles from Mason City—where Rosalie Willson had attended a funeral on one of the only two occasions she left Mason City. Howard flew in to the Mason City airport where arrangements had been made to drive him to Charles City.

The star of *The Andy Griffith Show, Happy Days*, and a number of movies arrived at the plant a few minutes before it opened. He chatted for several minutes with a security guard who did not recognize him. When the guard grew a bit suspicious and asked Howard what he was doing there, he explained that he was going to work there that day.

"Work here?" exclaimed the guard, looking at him from head to toe. "Boy, you better put some meat on those bones," he said.

Willson enjoyed one more success on Broadway. He wrote the book, music, and lyrics for a show entitled *Here's Love*, a stage adaptation of the hit 1947 film *Miracle on 34th Street*. The story is about a Santa Claus in Macy's Department Store who eventually has to prove in court that he is the real Santa Claus. The clincher comes when the post office hauls dozens of mail pouches into the courtroom, all packed with mail addressed to Santa Claus, and all delivered to the defendant. The defense wins its case because with the delivery of the mail, the U.S. government has in effect certified that the man on trial is indeed Santa Claus.

Willson filled the wondrous story with sprightly music. Not surprisingly, the play begins with a march and later on, Willson wowed the audience with what he called "the Adeste Fideles" march. Singer Janis

Paige had the female lead, playing a Macy's junior executive. Craig Stevens, better known at the time as television's "Peter Gunn," was the male lead, playing the lawyer who would eventually prove Santa was the real thing. Laurence Naismith played Kris Kringle. The show was directed by Stuart Ostrow.

Here's Love opened in Detroit at the Fisher Theater on August 9, 1963, with additional performances in Washington and Philadelphia before its carefully planned opening on Broadway. Like just about every show ever produced anywhere, problems were immediately apparent—and few escaped the notice of critics. "There are a number of things in *Here's Love* that are worthy of minor correction," chided Louis Cook in the *Detroit Free-Press*, who was acquainted with Willson from Cook's days at the *Des Moines* (Iowa) *Register*. "The show doesn't take off until several minutes after opening (the same problem Willson had to fix in *The Music Man* in Philadelphia), several of the lead voices showed the strain of heavy rehearsals, and it is obvious the key of some of the songs will have to be lowered." Cook wasn't finished. "Miss Paige's voice was almost inaudible during her big final number because she is so deep back stage. Some of the scenes are a little longer than they should be as is usually so in a musical in its early stages." Still, concluded the reviewer, "*Here's Love* will always be remembered as one of the magnificent tender creativities of our time, a time which has all too little tenderness."

The show played in Detroit for four weeks, long enough for Willson to move Miss Paige closer to the front of the stage for her big number and resolve some of the other problems. After more trial runs in Washington and Philadelphia, it opened on Broadway on October 3, 1963.

In Philadelphia, where reviewers enjoyed their reputations of being cutthroat critics, Willson was pleasantly surprised. "Let's skip the fancy preambles and get down to the facts of the case," announced the *Philadelphia Enquirer*, "which are that there is a happy show at the Shubert and that 'Music Man' Meredith Willson has done it again."

Time, as was its custom, was less than ecstatic about Willson's work. "It shouldn't happen to Macy's. It shouldn't happen to Gimbel's. And it certainly shouldn't happen to Santa Claus. The sorry, dispiriting news is that Meredith Willson has temporarily lost his '*Music Man*' bounce and '*Here's Love*' has all the festive gaiety of a lead balloon. This sentimental pap would not be so hard to swallow if it were sprinkled with a few laughs or spiced with a tingling score," continued the *Time* critic, "but 17 of the show's 21 scenes are over before a number comes alive that really rocks the house. . ."

Here's Love enjoyed a decent run of 334 performances. Ironically, the one song that emerged and captured the public's fancy was one Willson had written years before. He had snuck it into the show because it fit the theme so well. "It's Beginning to Look Like Christmas" grew to become not only a standard sung by millions of people each year, but also a popular phrase, one that Americans say each winter when they look out their window at the first snowfall.

In the summer of 1964, Willson took one more shot at network television in what promised to be a fun project. His old employer, NBC, signed him to do three hour-long specials. What made them truly "special" for Willson was that Rini was part of the package: they were going to do the shows together. As he prepared for the television specials, Willson told a reporter he had one goal in mind: "If you can't be funny, the rule is to be absorbing." He approached his television project with much more confidence and sophistication than he had 13 years earlier when the rules

Meredith and Rini perform during one of their summer 1964 NBC television specials. *MCPLA*

were to "spring on to the stage" and say frequently, "you're right, you're absolutely right." When asked to comment about his style, Willson said, "I guess I talk too much there on the stage. But people seem to like it. Our TV shows are an extension of our concert work, only more elaborate—and more absorbing, I hope."

The shows aired on June 30, July 28 and August 31, 1964. The first program had barely begun before Willson took a stab at pleasing the home folks. After spinning off one of his mawkish stories, he added, "That's the way we did it back in Mason City." Rini was also in fine form. She introduced Italian entertainer Caterina Valente and told the audience, "She will knock you down for a loop." The premiere show also featured a vamping Robert Preston, "The Young Americans" singing patriotic songs, and Sergio Franchi offering his extraordinary voice for a grateful audience.

But the guts of the entertainment was simply Willson as Willson. The Iowa native rattled through the "Trouble in River City" song, performed a powerful imitation of his hero John Philip Sousa leading a marching band, sang songs from *Molly Brown* and *Here's Love*, and for the finale, led a group of high school musicians marching across the stage playing "Seventy-Six Trombones" with its composer looking at the audience, pointing to the high school kids, and saying "God bless 'em."

Television was enjoyable—when it worked—but Willson developed a hankering to get back to Broadway, to put another production on stage. He had worked ceaselessly for five years on *The Music Man* and was 55 years old before it saw the light of day. Its stunning success hooked him. He could not escape Broadway's siren song, could not get the stage out of his mind. Even casual conversations on utterly unrelated topics would cause him to think about how to take whatever subject he was discussing, wrap it up in music, and deposit it on stage to entertain people.

In fact, it happened exactly that way one afternoon while he was chatting with an old friend, Ed Ainsworth, a columnist for the *Los Angeles Times.* Ed had just returned from a trip to Spain, where he had discovered, among other things, that the six-string Spanish guitar was invented 500 years earlier, in 1491. The conversation soon turned to the topic of a Willson musical based on the invention of the guitar. As the two men talked, Willson became preoccupied with the year 1491. "Something struck me about that date," he said later. "Wasn't some fellow doing something very important about that time?" Columbus, of course, was preparing to set out for his epic journey to the New World in 1492. Willson began thinking about what transpired the year before the adventurer set sail.

Willson's research discovered that the voyage of Columbus had been carefully chronicled from the time he left Spain on his long journey. Little, however, had been recorded prior to his departure. More research was required, and Willson was inclined to perform it himself. He had the time, the money, and a loving and supportive wife who wanted to go along. Within a short time he and Rini were on a plane bound for the Old World.

"I tried every avenue I could find," he later explained. "They were all unsatisfactory. But I wrote my play anyway." According to Willson, his research on Christopher Columbus found him to be energetic, enthusiastic, talkative, and inventive—much like Professor Harold Hill. Willson said Columbus's personality was a greater factor in convincing Spain's royalty to give him the *Nina*, *Pinta* and *Santa Maria* than any knowledge of the seas he may have possessed.

"Can I prove it? No, I can't prove '1491.' But I believe every word of it—and you can't prove I'm not right. We call it a Romantic Speculation."

Edwin Lester, head of the Los Angeles and San Francisco Civic Light Opera Companies, produced *1491*. Richard Morris, who wrote *The Unsinkable Molly Brown*, signed on as director. John Cullum, who starred with Barbara Harris in *On a Clear Day, You Can See Forever*, landed the starring role of Christopher Columbus. The play was scheduled to open in New York in January 1970. Willson was about to storm Broadway again.

The trial run for *1491* was at the Dorothy Chandler Pavilion in Los Angeles on September 3, 1969. James Powers, writing in the *Hollywood Reporter*, was not impressed. "1491 is a musical about Columbus' attempts to get his armada and get it sailing. Unhappily, this new Meredith Willson musical misses the boat. All three boats. The *Nina*. The *Pinta*. The *Santa Maria*. . . . It will not do for Broadway—if that was in anyone's mind."

Ironically, Powers criticized the play for lacking the very thing that Willson labored to include—background on what happened before Columbus set sail. According to the critic, "the trouble with '1491' is that it does not tell us what Columbus was like or what it is like to work and sweat and launch such an event, one to change the course of the world. It is as if, during the Apollo moon shot, the cameras had not been on the event itself but on Mrs. Astronaut at the Safeway." Powers' barbs stung, but they were just the beginning salvo in a string of negative reviews.

Dan Sullivan in the *Los Angeles Times* published a not-so-subtle warning for the play's producer. "Not for Broadway, Mr. Lester. There are sharks out there." Sullivan also directed a few direct words at Willson himself. "Meredith Willson's new musical about Columbus doesn't work," he stated without equivocation. "Not because it is hokum, (hokum can be fun) but because it is dull hokum. Just how dull is not at first apparent. It is clear from the opening curtain (a huge ancient map of the Atlantic; a spotlight picks up Spain and moves west) that the evening will not be a subtle one."

Sullivan recognized the similarity between Columbus and Harold Hill, but was not as fascinated with it as Willson. "It is clear from John Cullum's portrayal of Columbus as a proto-Prof. Harold Hill (selling doctored maps instead of trombones) that it will be a rather silly play." The review ended with a final insult: "I beg Willson to drop his experiments with opera and get back to writing tunes that people can whistle."

Willson had never been attacked so viciously in reviews. It was all the more disturbing because he had envisioned the Chandler Pavilion as giving him what he described as a "home field advantage." The critics' predictions, however, were generally on target. *1491* sailed off in September 1969 and was lost in a sea of bad reviews. It never made Broadway.

In the next five years, Willson toyed with writing a play about Jack London and with writing another of his stream-of-consciousness autobiographies. He no longer had the desire to write a Broadway show. "I'd just as soon not," he said. "I'd rather quit while I'm ahead. I see no necessity to take the risk of laying an egg to prove something I've already proven."

While the reviews of *1491* surely pained him, they were nothing to what he had endured during its development. Willson, who was honorary national chairman of the Easter Seal campaign, had appeared in a two-hour show in Des Moines in November 1966, to help kick off the state's Easter Seal campaign. Rini usually accompanied him, but this time she was conspicuously absent. She is not with me, he explained to the audience, because she is seriously ill. In fact, she was dying.

Rini had developed sarcoma, a form of cancer. The news devastated Meredith. After several months of suffering, Rini Willson died December 6, 1966, at St. John's Hospital in Santa Monica, California. The grief-stricken Willson said little publicly about the death of the woman he always referred to as "my Rini."

"There are many memories of Rini Willson here," commented an editorial in the Mason City *Globe-Gazette* three days after her death. "The most lasting picture is that of a smiling, outgoing lady at the side of her husband, Meredith Willson. Their affection was open and natural."

W. Earl Hall, writing recently about Meredith Willson, remembered the couple this way: "Musically and in all other ways, she has complemented Meredith in the pursuit of his career. On his early morning walks, he frequently comes up with a new tune. He has only to hum or whistle it to Rini and it is straightway set to paper. She is his most valued critic."

And now she was no more.

Rini was buried in Forest Lawn Cemetery in Glendale, California. On November 14, 1979, her body was reinterred in Elmwood Cemetery in Mason City. Meredith and his third wife, Rosemary, were present at the grave side service.

Rosemary Sullivan first met Meredith Willson in Detroit in 1941. At that time she was a young, vivacious, single woman when Willson came to town as guest conductor for the *Ford Evening Hour* with Eleanor Steber and Lanny Ross as guest soloists. Ford Motor Company was one of his sponsors on the west coast, so it was a natural to come to Detroit and do a guest spot in the home town of Cyril Bottom, a top Ford executive. (It was during his stay in Detroit that Willson committed the gaffe of telling Mrs. Bottom he remembered her name because he always connected a name with a face.)

Rosemary was a diehard Willson fan. She and her girlfriend went to the studio where the show was being broadcast and waited for him. When he emerged after the show to make his way to a cocktail party being thrown in his honor, Rosemary and friend approached him for his autograph. "We told him we were coming to California and that we sure would like to see his *Maxwell House* program. He said to call him when we got there," Rosemary later recalled. "Well, we were young and enthusiastic and so when we arrived in Los Angeles, we called NBC, called several times in fact, but he was never available."

Undaunted, the young women devised another plan. "There were things we wanted to do. We didn't want to just sit around a hotel room and try to keep calling. So we left a message for him to call us," explained Rosemary years later. "Imagine—a couple of girls from Detroit leaving a message for Meredith Willson to call us. We went sight-seeing, and when we got back to our hotel, there were several messages. One of them was from Meredith. He said if we got back before six o'clock, to go to the artist's entrance at NBC and there would be two tickets for us for the show."

Rosemary and her friend could not believe their ears—or their luck. "We got there so close to show time that there were no seats left. But the security guard said Meredith had left word to find seats for us somewhere. So we sat in the sponsors booth with all the sponsors and their wives and watched the show. We felt so out of place. We were in casual clothes

Rosemary Willson in 1988. She first met Meredith in 1941 and married him twenty-seven years later, two years after Rini's death. *Mason City Globe Gazette*

because we had no idea, of course, that this was going to happen or where we'd be sitting."

Rosemary later returned to California and found a job as a secretary at Monogram Studios, which became Allied Artists. Monogram produced films for Johnny Mack Brown and Jimmy Wakely, popular cowboy stars of the era. Still a fan of Willson and his music, Rosemary hung around the nearby NBC studios as often as she could.

The years passed and radio shows gave up ground to television. In addition to trying to conquer the new medium, Willson was also writing a play about a con man selling musical instruments that he hoped would someday play Broadway. When *The Music Man* hit it big, Willson was forced to spend much of his time in New York and employ a staff there. In 1958, he moved back to Los Angeles—and Rosemary Sullivan got a phone call.

"I'll never forget it. I was doing my laundry at the time. And this voice said, 'Do you know who this is?' And it was Meredith. He said his secretary had quit because she wanted to stay in New York rather than move to Los Angeles. So he needed a new secretary. And Rini said to him, 'What about that girl who is always hanging around?'"

And he remembered me and remembered my name and called me. And that's how I went to work for him," she said.

Rosemary took a six-month leave of absence from Monogram and signed on to work for Willson. The composer and his staff went to Europe for several months, however, and by the time they returned Rosemary's leave of absence was up. She was about to go back to her studio job when Willson hired her full-time. She remained with Willson until 1964, when she went to work for Universal Studios and then went to Paramount.

On Valentine's Day 1968, two years after Rini's death, Willson and Rosemary Sullivan were married. No one knew better or appreciated more than Rosemary the special bond that had existed between Meredith and Rini Willson.

Rosemary, a devoted wife and companion, learned to adjust to Meredith's rigid work schedule at home. "When he was working on a show, he would get up at around 5 a.m.," she later remembered. "He would go into his music room. When he was in there, if you wanted him for something, you didn't knock. You scratched on the door because that wasn't as likely to break his concentration."

Willson worked through the day. "He usually stopped work for the day at 6 o'clock in the evening so he could have dinner. Eventually, he built a studio and that's where he would work. There was an intercom in there but it was only to be used in emergencies," she said.

Rosemary did not possess the musical talent Rini had, and she knew it. Meredith knew it, too. When he played a new composition for Rosemary, he said he could tell by her facial expression whether she liked it. He also knew when she didn't like it, because she would always say, "Oh, that's nice, Meredith." Still, Willson appreciated Rosemary's opinion as a lay person because he believed it was people like her—fans, and not trained musicians—that he had to satisfy to keep his music popular.

"Silky Sullivan," he called her, the name of a popular race horse. They were married for 16 years.

Meredith and Rosemary with Art Swanson, Meredith's lifelong friend, in November 1972 on the Meredith Willson Footbridge in Mason City, Iowa. *Mason City Globe Gazette*

Chapter 13

"What song would you like to hear?"
— *Meredith Willson to the Enabnit children*

Cotton on the Elephant

eredith Willson enjoyed his celebrity status, but walked well in his own native skin when he returned home to Mason City to take part in civic activities and mingle with family and friends—"kissin' cousins," as he often called them. He also loved having fun with his audiences, be they large or small.

One of his subtle jests is found in *The Music Man*. Two of his most popular songs, "Seventy-Six Trombones" and "Goodnight My Someone," have exactly the same melody. The difference is that one is a march and the other is a love song sung almost like a lullaby. Willson never promoted the fact that the two songs were the same tune with different beats. In one of the famous scenes on the footbridge, Harold Hill sings "Seventy-Six Trombones" on one side of the bridge while Marian the Librarian begins to sing "Goodnight My Someone" on the other side. At one point, they switch and the professor sings part of the love song while the librarian sings the march. By accomplishing the counterpoint with two songs with the same melody, Willson was having a little fun with his audience.

Willson often found it difficult to pass up a chance to have a little fun with people, even if his audience consisted of just a single soul. In 1976, he stopped in at the office of Charles Walk, editor of the Mason City *Globe-Gazette.* Walk noticed that Willson, who was sporting a short-sleeved shirt, was wearing four watches—two on each wrist. The editor was unable to contain himself.

"Meredith, why are you wearing four wrist watches?"

"I often wear long sleeves or a coat," he replied, "so the four watches usually go unnoticed." Walk's question sparked an idea within Meredith.

"Let's have the newspaper hold a contest to see who could guess why I wear four watches," he suggested. He told Walk to send all the answers to him in California. "Rosemary and I will pick the best answer and send the winner a prize."

It wasn't until after Willson left the office that Walk realized the composer had never answered his question.

Walk conducted the contest with *Globe-Gazette* readers and the response was tremendous. All of the answers were forwarded to Meredith and Rosemary in California. The couple selected an entry and, true to his word, Meredith sent a special gift as first prize. The lucky winner was a woman from Rockford, Iowa, a neighboring town to Mason City. Her prize was a page from the original score of *The Unsinkable Molly Brown.*

Willson loved to stop in the *Globe-Gazette* offices whenever he visited Mason City and just sit and chat. He enjoyed a special friendship with editor Earl Hall. In fact, the barbershop quartet in *The Music Man* was patterned after "The Rusty Hinges," a barbershop group in Mason City that included Hall.

Willson also developed friendships with Hall's successors, Bob Spiegel, Chuck Walk, and Bill Brissee. "He was the damn-dest gabbber I ever met," recalls Walk with great fondness.

According to Walk, it was not unusual for Willson to pop in for a visit late in the afternoon. "He could talk for hours. When I saw him coming, I'd call my wife and tell her I would be late for dinner—Meredith's here— and she knew exactly what I meant."

Walk loves recalling Meredith's fun-loving personality. "One thing about Meredith—he could be talking to you and someone would walk by and he'd interrupt himself to say, 'ya know, that guy reminds me of so-and-so,' and he'd start talking about something else. Then he'd either return to the original conversation or start up on something new. I'd be sitting there thinking he's got three conversations going on at once with me—which one do I want to jump in on?"

Two subjects that were never out of Meredith's mind were his hometown and the New York stage. "He loved to talk about Mason City and Broadway," remembers Walk. "Those were his two favorite subjects. He often said he wished *Molly Brown* had gotten the same kind of accolades *The Music Man* got because he thought it was that good."

Rosalie Willson was also the topic of warm comments. "He talked a lot about his mother and not much about his father. And he hardly ever talked about Dixie," remembered the former *Globe Gazette* editor. "You could kind of tell that the relationship with Dixie was a little strained. I never felt that way about his relationship with Cedric. He and Cedric didn't see each other often but they got along well. Dixie could be a cold fish and she was pretty much of a 'me' person.

"But in all the years I knew Meredith, I never heard him say a bad word about anybody," continued Walk. "He simply wouldn't do it. In fact, he would go out of his way to say something nice about somebody." One example was John Philip Sousa. "Everyone knew Sousa was a tyrant to the people who worked for him. But Meredith talked about him like he was second father to him," explained Walk.

While Willson's conversations were lengthy, his letters were not. Walk recalls that a typical letter from him was handwritten and would say something like 'saw this' or 'liked this' and included a clipping from the *Globe-Gazette*. Occasionally, the newspaperman noted, he'd get a note from Willson with a newspaper clipping and a note that simply said, "'What were you thinking about?'"

One of the things many people close to Willson noticed was how the man's life changed through his relationship with his wives. Chuck Walk didn't know Peggy personally, but understood her to be a woman who stayed in the background. Rini, in contrast, was a performer and a good match because she and Meredith "seemed always to be on the same wave length, enjoying the same things, performing together, thinking together, living together, loving together."

"When Rini died, Meredith became almost reclusive," said Walk. "He had lost the love of his life and he was just devastated. Rosemary had known Willson since 1941 and had been his secretary for many years. She understood him and certainly understood the love he had for Rini."

"Rosemary," explained Walk,

> is a gracious lady and they had a wonderful marriage, a wonderful relationship. Even after they were married, she continued to be his appointment secretary in a sense. Sometimes she would come with him on his visits to the Globe. She would sit for a while and listen to him talk.

When she got bored, she'd get up, go out of the office and talk with other people. Then she would come back in and tell him that it was time leave or they'd be late for where ever they had to go next.

He and Rosemary had a tremendous marriage and relationship but it was different than Meredith's relationship with Rini and both of those had to be different than the relationship he had with his first wife. Rosemary understood all of this and filled an important void in Willson's life. They loved each other dearly.

Thirty-six years earlier in 1940, Willson, by then a successful composer and radio personality, returned to Mason City for a visit. Once back home, he indulged his urge to spend some time at one of his old haunts, Vance's Music Store. John Vance was delighted Meredith was in town and asked him to autograph records and sheet music of his number one hit, "You and I." Willson, of course, willingly complied. He enjoyed the opportunity to talk with hometown folks and sign music as much as anything. As he talked with customers, there was no hint of celebrity in him at all; he was just a hometown boy who had moved out west and was now home for a visit. Vance recalled that Willson not only signed the merchandise that day, but

Meredith plays the piano in one of his favorite Mason City hangouts, Vance's Music Store. Behind him are John Vance, Sr. and John Vance, Jr.
MCPLA

began selling it, too! He was doing so well he agreed to cover for the store clerk over the lunch hour.

While the employee was grabbing a bite to eat, Willson engaged in chit-chat with every customer who strolled in. Most were there because they needed to buy something. Some were simply old friends who wanted to talk with Meredith. Others were there to catch a glimpse of Mason City's favorite son. Willson entertained them all with his light and often hilarious banter. He sold a record to one woman and, as he was putting it in a sack for her, asked why she didn't go ahead and buy the sheet music too. The woman explained that she didn't own a piano. Willson engaged her in conservation for a while, and by the time the woman left, she owned the record, the sheet music—and a piano.

Another example of Willson's ability to mix his celebrity status with his homespun values is the day he called St. Joseph Mercy Hospital in Mason City from his home in Los Angeles. He told hospital personnel that he had just completed a composition and was so happy about it that he wanted to try to put some joy into someone else's life.

"Who could I call and play it for?" he asked. The staffer knew just the person.

Clair Reding of West Bend, Iowa, had been stuck in the hospital for a month recovering from injuries he had received in a serious auto accident. The call was put through, and Clair got the surprise of his life.

"You see things like this on television, not in real life. But it happened," said Reding. He said Willson played the song and told him to get well soon and return to his farm.

"It's planting time," Willson reminded him.

"It's probably the nicest thing that has ever happened to me," said Reding.

On each visit home, Willson would take time to see his friend from childhood, Art Swanson. The Swansons lived in the big house on the corner, about five houses north of the Willsons. Art was two years older than Meredith but age made no difference to them. As neighborhood pals they took hikes, rode bikes, played baseball together, and later, performed in the high school band. "We played on opposite ends of the scale," joked Willson. "Art played the tuba and of course I had my piccolo."

The pair were fast friends for almost 70 years, until Swanson died suddenly on Christmas Day 1977. Willson was unable to attend the funeral, but sent a glowing tribute of his friend to the *Globe-Gazette*. The following summer he flew home to Mason City and joined Swanson's son, Tom, and his wife, Ann, and their three children for dinner. One of the Swanson girls mentioned to him that she didn't have a grandpa anymore. "I'll be your grandpa," Willson told her. For the next few years, he sent her cards and gifts on birthdays and at Christmas time. The cards were always signed "Grandpa Meredith and Grandma Rosemary."

On another occasion, "Grandpa" helped one of the Swanson girls with a homework assignment. She wrote to him in California and asked him to write back, telling her some of his memories of his hometown. Instead of writing, Willson sent a tape recorded message. In it, he explained to her his method for getting thoughts on paper. He always jotted down his thoughts on a pad of paper with a felt pen, he explained. Then he played with those thoughts until he was satisfied with what he wanted to say. He had done that with this assignment, only instead of sending the final version in writing, he read aloud his thoughts into a tape recorder and sent it along to her.

Ted Enabnit, a Mason City attorney, met Willson in 1962 when Enabnit, as a member of the Junior Chamber of Commerce, was helping with the Band Festival. His job was to get parade participants lined up in their vehicles before the parade. He and Willson engaged in small talk as Enabnit went about his task. The young lawyer was a barbershop singer—something Willson could relate to—and had a relative who was a classmate of Willson's at Mason City High School. The conversation between the two men blossomed into a fine and lasting friendship.

Enabnit had two experiences with Willson that demonstrated both the celebrity and the down-to-earth nature of the man. On one occasion, Enabnit and his wife, Carol, were guests of Meredith and Rosemary at their home in Los Angeles. "Meredith bought Rosemary a Rolls Royce," recalled Ted. "They took us out to eat at Spike Jones' widow's restaurant. Rosemary drove. As soon as we came in the door of the restaurant, the band started playing Meredith's music. And that's all that they played all the time we were there."

Enabnit was obviously impressed with the treatment they received at the California eatery. "We had four waiters who did nothing but wait on us. Rosemary had a sheaf of five-dollar bills which she took out of her purse and handed to Meredith. He handed out the five-dollar bills to each waiter with each course of the dinner. He enjoyed the celebrity status and the things that it brought him, but at the same time, he never brushed anyone off. That's just the kind of person he was."

Not every man is able to buy his wife a Rolls Royce, one of the world's most expensive automobiles, and Willson took great pride in the fact that he could. And then he kidded about how he saved money with the purchase. "By buying a Rolls, I avoided having to purchase Rosemary's initial to put on the auto," he explained. "You know, R for Rosemary, R for Rolls. That saved anywhere from $3 to $17, depending on what kind of initial you have put on."

The Willson home in southern California was, in many respects, a music museum. As Enabnit remembers it: "At his home, he had just put a large addition onto his house for his studio. It had two large grand pianos which were in there back to back. The walls of the studio were filled with mementoes of his career. In another part of the house was his old office and studio, and just off of that was a bathroom, a half-bath. The walls of that little bathroom were filled with autographed pictures of many of the famous people he knew—Bob Hope, Bing Crosby—each picture signed and with a little note to Meredith."

An evening at the Enabnit home. (From left to right): Ted Enabnit, Rosemary Willson, Cedric Willson, Meredith Willson, holding Brian, Lois Willson, Cedric's wife, holding Kevin, and Carol Enabnit. *Ted Enabnit*

Willson was a dinner guest of the Enabnits during one of his visits home. After the meal, Willson went into the living room and sat down at a piano. Two Enabnit children, Kevin, age 6, and Brian, age 4, stood beside him as he played.

"What song would you like to hear?" he asked the youngsters.

Little Brian said excitedly, "Cotton on the Elephant" and said it in a manner as if everyone would know what he was talking about, as if he had said "America the Beautiful" or "Row, Row, Row Your Boat."

Willson didn't miss a beat. With a simple smile spread comfortably across his face, he ran his fingers up and down the keyboard. Within a minute or two he had a melody, and a few moments later, lyrics. And that is how Brian and Kevin—and their parents—became the first to hear Willson's newest song, "Cotton on the Elephant."

Carol Enabnit snapped a picture of the two boys and Willson at the piano that night. And he has it to this day. About ten years later, both boys were all-state musicians in the high school band, Brian as a euphonium player and Kevin as a percussionist. Both were awarded music scholarships to the University of Iowa.

Sometimes when Willson returned to Mason City, his brother Cedric joined him. The two men led separate, busy lives and because of this, they were not close in the sense of keeping close track of one another. But they were proud of each other's accomplishments, cordial to one another, and had a good time together whenever their paths crossed.

Ted Enabnit was responsible for one of those reunions. The busy attorney was also the chairman of a fund-raising campaign to build a community auditorium in Mason City. He quickly enlisted the help of Meredith and Cedric Willson. The brothers were eager to do anything they could to help their hometown with such a worthwhile project, and both made a special trip home for a fund-raising rally in September of 1974.

The siblings drove together to see their old high school building, which held fond and warm memories for both of them. Once inside the school, the brothers soon found themselves inside the auditorium. With Cedric at his side, Meredith ambled in his easy, smooth style to the center of the stage and looked out toward the balcony. "I just had to see this place where I received my diploma," said Meredith. "Right here in this spot in 1919. I was to make a speech and was totally unprepared. I was trembling like a leaf until I looked down and saw Reuben Nyquist. He clenched a fist as a sign of encouragement and, thanks to him, I got away with a short

Meredith plays his piccolo while brother Cedric enjoys the performance from the stage at the old high school. Cedric said Meredith was smart all of the time and that he was smart once—when he decided not to be a musician. The pair were back home helping raise money for the North Iowa Community Auditorium. *MCPLA*

speech." Unlike Willson, who had left Mason City to make his career in music, Nyquist remained in his hometown and taught for 39 years in the Mason City school system. He died in 1972.

Cedric, who even as a child was the more practical of the two brothers, stood on the stage next to Meredith and reflected on his days as a musician. Meredith's brother always played down his musical talent, but those who knew him well also knew he was good enough to play the bassoon for a year with the Sousa band at the same time his brother was playing the piccolo.

"Meredith was smart a lot of times. I was smart once," Cedric explained. "When we were on the Sousa band, we talked about what to do between seasons. Meredith decided to stay. I decided to go back to school. They were smart moves for both of us." At that, both brothers broke into a joyous laughter that echoed through the largely empty hall.

Meredith fully appreciated Cedric's musical talents and took a moment that day, as both stood on the stage that is now no more, to underscore the fact by pointing out how Cedric used a bit of foolproof Sousa jargon. "If someone tells you he was in the Sousa band, walk away," said Meredith. "As Cedric said, he was 'on' the Sousa band. I don't know why. That's just the way it was."

At the fund-raising banquet, the brothers did what everyone there expected them to do. Meredith rallied the troops with engaging chit-chat that blended his Hollywood celebrity status with his "gee whiz, it's good to be back here with you folks" type of conversation. Cedric, meanwhile, who was vice president of Texas Industries in Dallas, Texas, looked over the plans for the new building with the eye of an expert. "You know, I'm a nit-picker—and they look pretty good to me," he said.

The fund-raising campaign was a smashing success, and Meredith was invited to the ground breaking ceremony. He enjoyed the honor of lifting out the first shovel of Iowa dirt. Thanks to the help of the Willsons and scores of other dedicated Iowa residents, the North Iowa Community Auditorium has been hosting dramas, musical performances, political forums, and guest speakers for Mason City and surrounding communities for 25 years.

Whenever Mason City friends visited the Willsons in Los Angeles, the couple often took them out to dinner. When the Willsons came back to Mason City, they usually ate at the homes of the friends. A typical dinner included Iowa pork chops, corn on the cob, and pie (Willson loved homemade pie) and then everyone would gather around the piano for

Meredith breaks ground at the site of the new North Iowa
Community Auditorium. *MCPLA*

some light entertainment and laughter. It was a long way from the hustle
and bustle of Hollywood and its glitter and movie stars and fancy
restaurants and Rolls Royces—a lifestyle that Willson fit into just fine and
enjoyed when he was there. But when he made his trips back to Mason
City—and marched in the Band Festival, stopped in at Vance's Music Store
to shoot the breeze like he had as a kid and sell sheet music and a piano,
stroll on the footbridge with his old friend Art Swanson, and eat corn on
the cob and apple pie—Meredith Willson was home.

Meredith and Rosemary Willson in 1981. *MCPLA*

Chapter 14

"He was the personification of light . . . not darkness.
He was a giver of joy . . . not despair."

— Ken Kew, Mayor, Mason City, Iowa

May the Good Lord Bless and Keep You . . .

Meredith Willson received honors and recognition from four presidents. In 1962, President John F. Kennedy presented the National Big Brother Award to him in ceremonies at the White House in recognition of his devotion to the cause of youth in America. Willson, who did not have any children, was a six-time president of the Big Brothers of Greater Los Angeles, a private, non-profit, non-sectarian agency that provided support, through positive role models, to fatherless boys between the ages of 6 and 12 through a variety of mentoring programs.

In 1966, President Lyndon Johnson named him to the National Council of Humanities, an appointment that was challenged by 70 college professors who signed a letter of protest and mailed it to the White House. Professor Arthur Mendel of Princeton University was the spokesman for

President John F. Kennedy presents Meredith Willson with a
National Big Brother Award at the White House in 1962 while a
proud Rini looks on. MCPLA

the protesting professors, all of whom were music teachers. Mendel was not
impressed with Willson's accomplishments with his plays and popular
music.

"These things are enterprises designed to make money, do not need
government support, and are unrelated to the purposes of the act," he
complained, referring to the purpose for which the council was
created—to provide government support, where needed, to the arts.

Other members of the council were Dr. Henry Allen Moe, chairman,
president of the American Endowment for the Humanities; I. M. Pei, a
noted architect; Dr. Robert Goheen, president of Princeton University;
Emily Gensuer, art critic of the *New York Herald-Tribune*; the Rev. John
Courtney Murray, a Roman Catholic theologian; and Dr. Kenneth Clark,
professor of psychology at the City College of New York.

"It's not for me to say whether I am or am not qualified," said Willson. When asked if he would respond directly to the letter, he said he would not. "That will have to come from President Johnson or his advisers," he answered. "I did not apply for the spot on the council. I was chosen for reasons best known by the president or his advisers and that is why I feel any reply should not come from me." President Johnson defended the appointment and Willson remained on the council, which was largely a ceremonial position.

Willson was still doing concerts around the country, but they were different than the ones he and Rini used to do. Rosemary was a devoted wife and companion, but she was not a performer. While Rini's place was on stage standing beside Meredith, Rosemary's was in the first or second row of the audience, where her presence was a source of great support for him.

Willson was in such demand for Fourth of July celebrations that he hired an agency, W. Colston Leigh, to book the concerts for him. Rosemary has fond memories of those days:

> We used to travel for about a week, just on Fourth of July appearances. He'd conduct the orchestra and he ended each concert with 'The Stars and Stripes Forever.' Meredith always said that was one sure way to get an encore.
>
> At the end of his concerts, he'd start to reminisce with the audience and he'd get going telling some of his old stories. Sometimes, it would get to be 11 o'clock. I'd be sitting in the audience and members of the orchestra, who were behind Meredith, would look at me and point to their watches. I'd shrug my shoulders. I mean, what did they think I could do about it?

By the early 1970s, Willson, nearing the age of 70, had reached the time in his life when he was beginning to feel the need to slow down. He began noticing aches and pains in his arms, shoulders, and back—particularly after his first rehearsals, he said. "They were more noticeable than ever," was how he put it.

But he hadn't lost his flair for sitting down and writing a song. In 1972, he took up the task of composing a march for the Shriners organization. "All those bands, and they don't have a march!" he exclaimed to his old friend Art Swanson. "Well, they do now."

In 1974, President Gerald Ford asked him to come up with a theme song for the president's "WIN" program, an acronym for "Whip Inflation Now." The offer surprised and flattered him. "I was very thrilled, very inspired," said Willson. "It is the commission of a work that has always inspired the artist—and the higher the commission, the greater the inspiration." The march he produced, he once explained, was as a song of encouragement. "There's a battle against inflation, and in that respect, it's a war song." When asked if his work for the president constituted a political commitment, responded, "I walk the middle path. I vote the man, I guess, rather than the party."

The late 1960s and early 1970s were colored with misery for the Willson family. In February of 1968, Cedric Willson's son, Army Captain Lloyd Meredith Willson, was killed in Vietnam. Willson, 27, was a career Army officer, having received a commission after graduating from the University of Kansas in 1962. He went to Vietnam in August of 1967 and was awarded the Air Medal for flying helicopter missions before transferring to a combat unit. He was serving with the 16th Infantry, 1st Division, when he was killed during a field operation. In addition to his parents and two sisters, Captain Willson left behind a wife and daughter in Dallas. Unfortunately, Lloyd Willson's death was just the first of a string of tragedies.

On February 6, 1974, Dixie Willson died in Fair Haven, New Jersey, at the age of 83. Friends and acquaintances claimed Meredith's relationship with his sister had been strained for almost 20 years. One close family friend described the siblings as being "estranged." Certainly it was not the same relationship the pair once shared when the loving and caring sister showed her wide-eyed, teenaged brother the sights of New York City almost six decades earlier. Rosemary Willson, however, said that when Dixie became seriously ill, Meredith went to see her and kept in contact with her doctors. After she died, he wrote a tribute to her that was published in the *Globe-Gazette*. His words, though, were noticeably void of sentiment. "Dixie knew she had talent. And with that knowledge, she had the courage of a lioness in putting it to work. Examples are legion," he wrote.

Within a year Willson was eulogizing his brother. Cedric Willson died of a heart attack in Dallas on January 10, 1975. He was 74. Cedric's passing left Meredith the sole surviving member of the family. The grief-stricken composer called Chuck Walk, the editor of the *Globe-Gazette*, to talk about the passing of his older brother:

> A kid brother oftener than not is a pain in the neck and I certainly was
> no exception. My brother, Cedric, never said a testy word to me, nor
> did he ever fail to listen sympathetically to my youthful petulances. His
> patient understanding in facing crises was never-failing. He was the
> quietly courageous kind. I know. I've seen him hang on to his 'cool'

when I was frightened to death. The four most understated words describing Cedric are: "He will be missed."

Willson had been an unswerving patriot in word and deed for all of his adult life, and had always managed to remain above and beyond politics. In 1980, he made an exception. When an old friend and fellow transplanted Midwesterner, Ronald Reagan decided to run for president, Willson unabashedly supported him and paid for radio commercials that he made on his behalf before the Iowa caucuses. He also gave him permission to use "76 Trombones" as one of his campaign theme songs.

Unofficially retired but still in great demand, Willson traveled across the country with Rosemary to take part in various activities involving him or his music. In 1979, they flew to Detroit to participate in a tribute to John Phillip Sousa, the great bandmaster who gave Willson his first big break in New York fifty-eight years earlier. At one point in the celebration, Willson was asked to come forward and lead the band in the playing of "76 Trombones." One pair of eyes in the audience belonged to Sousa's grandson, John Philip Sousa III. "It was Goose pimple-ville," Willson jested afterwards.

Age was catching up with the unsinkable Music Man. Care was taken to make certain his public events were no more strenuous than necessary. Two exceptions were his appearance in Minneapolis in 1981, and at the Rose Bowl game in 1982, when the University of Iowa played the University of Washington. In Minneapolis, Willson led a band of 2,700 musicians who had assembled to kick off the city's Business Salutes The Arts Week. The huge band, made up of 30 Minnesota high school bands, augmented by musicians from the University of Minnesota, occupied three blocks of downtown Minneapolis.

Frank Bencriscutto, the university's band director, was the main director for the event. He stood in the cherry picker of a truck and directed with a baton equipped with a flashlight. Thirty other directors, scattered among the band members, helped direct. The weather ball on the nearby Northwestern National Bank flashed in one-quarter time segments. Willson directed the final number, "America the Beautiful," but opted to do it from the ground rather than above the musicians in the cherry picker.

The Minneapolis affair earned Willson and the other participants a spot in the *Guinness Book of World Records*. No one had ever led a larger

Meredith strikes a familiar pose as he leads the University of Iowa Band in the "Iowa Fight Song," which he wrote. *Mason City Globe Gazette*

band. The previous record was a contingent of 1,976 musicians from Virginia who played in President Richard Nixon's second inaugural parade. Guinness officials were on hand to witness the record-breaking feat. It was, at age 79, another first for Willson.

At the Rose Bowl in Pasadena, California—just a handful of miles from his home—Willson led the Hawkeye band in a stirring rendition of the "Iowa Fight Song," which he wrote in 1951. The band played in "platoons" because Rose Bowl rules allowed a maximum of 196 musicians on the field

Meredith enjoys a hearty laugh during a newspaper interview in Mason City on May 15, 1978, just three days before his 76th birthday. He took advantage of every opportunity he could during his visits home to see as many friends and fans as possible. *Mason City Globe-Gazette*

Meredith during a visit home in May 1978. His trips home were something he always looked forward to.   *Mason City Globe Gazette*

at one time. The Hawkeye band had 279 musicians, four twirlers, and 38 flag bearers. Band directors devised the platooning so everyone got to perform, even for just a moment, under Willson's direction. It was an opportunity none of them would ever have again.

Friends began to notice signs of ill health. During a visit to Mason City in 1983, Meredith looked frail and was sometimes disoriented. He stopped in at the *Globe-Gazette* to visit editor Bill Brissee and reporter Tom Thoma in Brissee's office. The trio had talked for several minutes about a variety of issues when Brissee mentioned to Thoma that they should do an interview and story with Willson while he was there. Thoma excused himself, left the editor's office for a moment, and returned with a notebook and pen. When he reentered the office, Willson stood up, looked at Tom, and asked, "Well, who is this fine-looking young man?"

During the same visit to Mason City, Meredith attended a picnic at a nearby farm. During the meal, he leaned over and asked a friend, "What's the name of this restaurant?"

In the spring of 1984, Willson began work on another project. This time he was helping with a new musical called *That Music Man's Music*, produced by Robert Jani and scheduled to open October 23 in Los Angeles. As he had all of his life, Willson once again associated himself with a distinguished coworker. Jani was an accomplished producer of lavish shows who previously had jobs with Radio City Music Hall and Disneyland. Willson had first met Jani in 1958, when *The Music Man* was still going strong on Broadway. At that time, Jani was producing the half-time shows at UCLA football games and had put together a spectacular presentation based on *The Music Man*. The pair became close friends.

On June 8, 1984, Willson became ill with an intestinal obstruction and was admitted to St. John's Hospital in Santa Monica. He initially responded to treatment and seemed to be making progress toward a full recovery. A week later, on Saturday, June 16, the *Mason City Globe-Gazette* was preparing a front-page splash about the retirement of publisher Jerry Moriarity, with a back at his long career in journalism. Their plans were interrupted by a news flash from the west coast:

> SANTA MONICA, Calif. (AP): Meredith Willson, the composer whose Broadway smash *The Music Man* set generations of toes tapping to "76 Trombones," died Friday night a hospital spokeswoman said. He was 82. He died at 8:30 p.m. of apparent heart failure, she said. His wife, Rosemary Patricia Sullivan was at his side.
>
> "I was with him and I must say, he went peacefully," said Rosemary. "It was very unexpected, really, but he did go peacefully. He just went to sleep. We thought we'd be home in a few days because they were clearing it up, but last night when he took a turn for the worse, his heart just gave way on him."

Stars, directors, producers and fans from around the world spoke out to offer words of comfort and remember the man who had touched their lives in so many ways. Robert Preston, Willson's star in *The Music Man* on both stage and screen, was stunned when he learned the news. "For me, he's never going to be dead. I've got him on the screen. I've got him on the record album. I've got him in my head. I hope he heard me say something loving about him last week on the Tony awards."

Debbie Reynolds, who was Molly Brown in the movie, said, "He and his music will be greatly missed. Those of us that performed his music did it with joy."

University of Iowa President James Freedman paid tribute to Willson, who did not attend Iowa or any other university, but who wrote the "Iowa Fight Song" and led the band at the Rose Bowl in 1982. "His memory will live through his music which brought joy to millions," he said, "as well as through the scholarship that he and Mrs. Willson so generously established for music students at the university."

Rosemary made arrangements for Willson's funeral to be in his beloved Mason City, followed by his burial in the family plot in Elmwood Cemetery. On Sunday, the day after news of his death was made public, 400 mourners attended a requiem mass at St. Martin of Tours Church in Los Angeles. There, John Green, a fellow conductor, composer and musician spoke of the loss of his friend:

> Thank you, Meredith, for bringing joy and beauty to our world while setting us a quiet but eloquent example of how life should be lived. Meredith had honesty, integrity, gracious gentility, simplicity, unpretentious elegance, generosity, caring, a never-failing sense of humor, the genuine humility and child-like lack of guile that Christ so wanted for all of us. . . . Good night, our Meredith, sleep tight, our Meredith, sweet dreams be yours. May you walk with sunlight shining and a bluebird in every tree. May God bless you and keep you till we meet again.

Services were held first in Los Angeles and then in Mason City at the First Congregational United Church of Christ—the same church his mother had taught Sunday School in for more than 30 years, and the same church Willson worshiped in when he visited Mason City and donated $50,000 toward the building of the Rosalie Reiniger Willson educational wing.

"We're thinking today of a vivacious man, but gentle; a proud man, but humble; a high-spirited man, but one who loved his church," said the Rev. Robert L. Stone. "Meredith was unique but kind. Meredith lived his life in his own particular impossible-to-duplicate style. He was a sucker for anyone who asked him for help. He was Iowa stubborn but he was also Iowa generous."

As the congregation, which included Iowa Governor Terry Branstad, rose to sing "Now Thank We, All Our God," Reverend Stone reminded the audience that this was one that Meredith could really "belt out." The music also included a medley of Willson's songs, including "76 Trombones," which opened and closed the service, "Till There Was You," "Wells Fargo Wagon," and "Goodnight My Someone."

Mason City Mayor Kenneth Kew, a former local radio and television personality, delivered a fine and apt tribute to the city's native son:

> Mason Citians have always been happy when our special native son, Meredith Willson, came back home. So today, I see no reason why we shouldn't be happy too. Meredith Willson was not the kind of man who would want his friends to be sad. He was the personification of light . . . not darkness. He was a giver of joy . . . not despair. The very fact that Rosemary has brought him home again is clear evidence that she was acutely aware of his love for his hometown and its people. A noted author is remembered for the phrase, "You can't go home again." Meredith proved you can go home . . . again and again and again.
>
> This city and this church were both home to Meredith. He lived in Mason City for the first 17 years of his life . . . and his beloved mother Rosalie was a Sunday School teacher in this church and is remembered by many of us. It's obvious that Meredith had nothing but pleasant memories of his life in this community. You can point to the many times that he elected to come back for a visit. A number of times it was by invitation . . . and many other times it was just because he wanted to.
>
> He was always welcomed with open arms. He was a small town boy who became famous worldwide but who never changed his manner. Meredith was proud to claim his roots in Mason City and Iowa.
>
> Everybody in this city knew Meredith. Just ask them. That indicates to me the pride our people have in letting the world know that he was one of us and that Meredith knew all of us. If he couldn't call you by name, you were "cousin." No one in this world had more cousins that Meredith Willson.
>
> Meredith was a talented man, but he was more than that. He was kindly, patient, unassuming, determined, cooperative and God fearing. He loved to sing hymns—even though he would never have won any awards for his vocal abilities.
>
> Our music man was never critical of anyone or anything other than himself. He was Iowa stubborn. It took him years to write and rewrite *The Music Man* before it was finally ready to appear on Broadway. All he succeeded in doing was capturing the hearts of an entire nation. Here was a Broadway show that was funny, had some of the finest music ever written and, believe it or not, was wholesome. Meredith never had to resort to profanity or sex in any of his projects.
>
> Mason City gave Meredith the background and the characters for *The Music Man*. And Meredith gave Mason City lasting national

attention as the original River City. One of the biggest events ever held here was the national press premiere of the movie version of *The Music Man*. It was held in conjunction with the annual North Iowa Band Festival in 1962. The city hosted Meredith, Robert Preston, Shirley Jones, Ronny Howard, Arthur Godfrey, Hedda Hopper and media representatives from across the country.

Our residents also showed their Iowa hospitality by providing housing in private homes for members of 100 high school bands representing various sections of the United States. They appeared here for a national marching competition.

Who can ever forget Meredith Willson in one of those Band Festival parades, as he climbed out of his official car, grabbed a huge baton from a surprised high school drum major, and merrily led the parade.

Who can forget the music composed by our music man? Back in the forties, he had two numbers ranked at the same time among the top ten popular tunes as presented by the national radio show, *The Lucky Strike Hit Parade*. We still sing regularly in this church, and will again today, "May the Good Lord Bless and Keep You."

And of course, from Meredith, the public always recognizes his Music Man hits . . . "Trouble in River City." "Marian the Librarian," "Till There Was You," and that tremendous counterpoint writing of "Goodnight My Someone" and "76 Trombones." To me, every time I hear "76 Trombones" thundering, thundering . . . I get chills of pride.

Meredith wrote other Broadway music, he authored a number of books, he wrote the fight songs for the University of Iowa and Mason City High School. He took time to travel and he received honors from institutes of higher learning. He was greatly admired by his peers. Meredith never ran out of projects. He just ran out of time. Meredith is off on a new adventure . . . and we should be happy for him. His spirit and his music will live forever in the hearts of all of us here in River City.

From this day forward, whenever I hear thunder rolling across the sky like tympanies and bass drums, I'll say to myself: There goes Meredith. He's leading another big parade.

The bronze-colored casket was draped in purple with a flower arrangement that included an emblem of a trombone. The funeral procession, on its way to Elmwood Cemetery, drove to the old homestead on Superior (now Pennsylvania) Avenue, stopping in front of the yard where Dixie, Cedric, and Meredith had put on performances, and where Rosalie greeted her kindergartners and was always on the lookout for mistreated animals. A barbershop quartet sang, and several characters from the Community Theater appeared, dressed in costumes from their most recent production of *The Music Man*. At the end of the singing, quartet members doffed their hats to Mrs. Willson, who blew them kisses and wiped tears from her eyes as the procession moved on to the cemetery.

A reception was held in the Congregational church basement after the service, a time for the people of Mason City—the subjects of Willson's hokey, corny, and loving Iowa humor—to share their favorite stories about the man who made their hometown famous. Gil Lettow, band director at Mason City High School, told the story of when Willson walked into a band rehearsal unexpectedly and unannounced. A startled but pleasantly surprised Lettow introduced him to his students as "Mr. Willson."

"He put up his hand as if to wave me off and said, 'call me Meredith.' He asked us, 'What are you working on?' He was extremely easy to visit with. It was an event those students and I will remember for a lifetime," recalled Lettow with fondness.

Blanche Lyng recalled a time Willson impacted her family by something he said. Her husband was reading the newspaper one evening and listening to the radio when Willson said, "Drop that newspaper and listen to me." "He dropped it like a ton of bricks," she laughed.

One of Iowa's most popular and famous newspaper columnists of the day was Chuck Offenburger, who penned a column called "Iowa Boy" for the *Des Moines Register*. Offenburger drove to Mason City in September, two months after Willson died, to visit his grave. A business trip had prevented him from attending the funeral. I had never met Willson, he explained, "But I had to say my good-byes." Offenburger wondered why the man and his music had such an impact on him:

> Perhaps what Willson gave me were directions on how to love Iowa," he wrote. "Appreciate its straight-arrow traditions. Tolerate its stubbornness. Exult in its neighborliness. Laugh out loud at Iowa, sure, but always with a genuine smile in the heart, not a sneer. . . . Hey, that may be it. That's probably why I was so taken by the man and his work, because even in real life, I'm nothing more than a Meredith Willson character—an Iowan. There, I've found my peace.

In 1952, Willson explained to a national radio audience how he'd like to be remembered. In a broadcast with CBS commentator Edward R. Murrow, he paid tribute to a departed friend who taught him that fame and fortune are fleeting, but kindness is everlasting. "I guess the creed of all human beings," explained Willson,

> embraces the desire to leave their mark on the mortal world when they pass to the immortal one. Many men feel a fervent need to leave a son to carry on their name; non-creative people envy the Shakespeares and the Beethovens as draftsmen envy the Frank Lloyd

Wrights and as the commercial artist envies the Rembrandts and the Raphaels. Maybe it's this kind of frustration that caused Henry David Thoreau to remark, 'The mass of men live lives of quiet desperation.'

Well, I had a friend by the name of Max Terr. And Max taught me that genius is by no means an essential for escape from this 'quiet desperation.' Max had been associated with me as choral director for the past 20 years or so. Max was interested in almost everything and, considering that he was also a perfectionist, his interest was always a very intense one . . . even if it was only in a pencil.

Being a composer and orchestrator, he was constantly writing at the piano and he could see no reason to live with a clumsy pencil or a bad light . . . so he puttered and he searched until he found a graceful, dependable, thoroughly efficient pencil and a fine light for his work, completely comfortable and satisfactory in every respect. Now Max very casually included his friends in this continuous research of his, and no one who knew Max ever took any of his suggestions lightly.

Since Max has gone, not a day passes that isn't a pleasanter day because of the things he left behind him. I have his particular kind of pencil in every pocket of every suit, and on the desk, on the night table and on the piano.

We have the world's greatest cookies at our house which Max sent one Christmas, after shopping all over town to find the best items to include in a basket for us. In every room of our apartment, there are memories of Max Terr. And lots of our friends swear by his patiently discovered items, passing them along to their friends—praising Maxie's cookies, Maxie's music paper, Maxie's pencils . . . and piano light—without ever having known Max Terr.

"So I guess I believe pretty firmly that you don't have to be a Beethoven or a Rembrandt, or even a father, to leave a heritage to the mortal world," Willson concluded. "This is not a creed exactly . . . nor is it a complete personal objective . . . or is it? Anyhow, I think if I leave behind me any part of the kind of things that keep Max Terr alive in the hearts of his fellows, I will have justified my brief hour of strutting and fretting upon the stage."

Elizabeth "Peggy" Van Bomel, Meredith's first wife, died on October 23, 1986, in New York City. She was 85. Peggy bequeathed to her brother, Ralph Wilson, eight percent of the fair market value of the principal of a trust fund she had established. He died less than a year later, on September 26, 1987. The trust to which he was a partial beneficiary amounted to approximately $2,000,000 and constituted only a tiny fraction of the Van Bomel estate.

Meredith Willson's final resting place in Elmwood Cemetery, Mason City, Iowa.
Photo by Dan Bjerke

Peggy's ashes were flown to Mason City for interment in Elmwood Park Cemetery. Loved ones who made the arrangements flew into town and returned home the same day.

In 1988, four years after his death, Meredith Willson was awarded the Presidential Medal of Freedom, the highest honor that can be bestowed upon an American citizen. Rosemary Willson accepted the award from President Reagan on behalf of her late husband.

Meredith Willson
1902 - 1984

"Willson had one masterpiece in him and it will live as long
as there is anything like musical theater."

— *Jay Nordlinger*, National Review

The 77th Trombone

*I*t is July 2000, the hot, sticky time of year in Mason City when humidity is uncomfortable during the day and mosquitoes are a nuisance at night.

In a little room in the archives at the Mason City Public Library, just across the street from Meredith Willson's boyhood home, Karla Jurgemeyer sits at a wooden table with stacks of notebooks, file folders, and assorted papers spread out in front of her. Every day for several weeks, she has trudged into this room, sat down at the table, opened her laptop computer and combed through the files. Karla is a graduate student from the University of Cincinnati, and she is writing her Master's thesis on *The Music Man* and its contributions to the world of music. It is the same room in which Andy Mast, a graduate student from the University of Iowa, did research for his Master's thesis earlier in this same year on the musical heritage of Mason City, focusing in part on the music of Meredith Willson.

Forty-three years after *The Music Man* premiered on Broadway and sixteen years after Willson's death, the radiance of his life and his music remain a part of the American culture, like a 77th trombone that keeps playing long after the big parade has passed by.

Each year, the *Globe-Gazette* receives requests from high school music and drama teachers from all over the country. The request is always the same: the drama or music department is putting on *The Music Man* as the school play and the director wants an issue of the *Globe*—any issue is fine. There is a scene in the musical in which Professor Harold Hill is reading a newspaper, and the director wants to use the "River City" newspaper as a prop.

In New York in April 2000, a revival of *The Music Man* opened on Broadway to glowing reviews. This time around, it was not like 1957 at all. Nobody had to put on midnight auditions in the homes of skeptical producers and directors. Nobody scoffed at the corny Iowa humor. There was no problem finding financial backers. "In an age of Broadway musicals so impersonal that one of their most frequent sources of new material is old movies, *The Music Man* is a reminder of another time in musical-theater history, when melodious ideas for the stage were as organically grown as cornfields, when showy spectacles could be teased out of the experiences of a single life," Peter Marks wrote in *The New York Times*. *USA Today* praised the revival and commented that "Meredith Willson was the star of the show."

Across the street from the Mason City library, the Meredith Willson boyhood home at 314 S. Pennsylvania Avenue is now open for tours. On the second floor is the little room where Meredith went to bed each night, looked out the window, and dreamed of one day playing in John Phillip Sousa's band. Down the street about five houses south is Willow Creek, the body of water Rosalie Willson tried to have renamed as a river 80 years earlier—an act that inspired her son to use the name "River City."

Next door to the birthplace is Music Man Square, a magnificent $10,000,000 museum and conservatory, built entirely with state grants and private funds—and with generous matching funds donated by Rosemary Willson. It is a lasting tribute to the man whose music is still heard all over the world, but who started making it on Pennsylvania (Superior) Avenue in Mason City nearly a century ago. Engraved in the concrete across the top of the building, facing downtown Mason City, are the words: "Seventy-six Trombones Led the Big Parade."

Willson had an unassuming attitude about the fame and fortune he achieved. He said once, "I'm still trying to write something by way of music that might have a chance of lasting longer than I do."

The legacy has taken fascinating twists and turns. In 1979, Harry Levins of the *St. Louis Post-Dispatch* wrote a piece that involved a conversation between two men at a bar talking about the upcoming presidential election in 1980, and how the media would be hustling to get the pulse of the nation.

"Every time some editor in the east wants to know what America is thinking, he tells somebody to get to the Midwest," said one of the characters. "And whoever he sends seems to end up in Hannibal or Mason City. Why is that?" he wondered.

"That's easy," explained his companion. "Hannibal, Missouri, is a natural because it's the home of Tom Sawyer. And as for Mason City," he said, "that's River City, the home of "Seventy-Six Trombones.""

"Back in the days when Philadelphia was the home of the *Saturday Evening Post*, Norman Rockwell made a good part of his living by painting scenes set in places like Hannibal and Mason City," the man continued. "The editors at the *Post* loved it. We all know that isn't what America is like. But that's what we like to think it's like."

And the legacy continues. In 1995, a library in Virginia started an "adults only" section of its library because some community residents found contents of some books objectionable and did not want them within the reach of children. The removal spawned another reaction, this one from residents who thought the library had overreacted. The *Washington Post*, in reporting and commenting on the story, sought an outside opinion. The newspaper contacted Andrew "Andy" Alexander, the librarian in Mason City, Iowa—River City. That is an example of the stature given to the library and to the legacy of the man who created the image. Alexander told the *Post* reporter that in Mason City, "it's everybody's library with no one viewpoint. You can quote me, Marian the Librarian," he said.

The legacy reaches far and wide and spans decades. Shortly after the opening of the Broadway revival of *The Music Man*, columnist Don Freeman in the *San Diego Union-Tribune* felt the need to inform readers who might be too young to remember Willson: "The man could do it all. He could write a powerhouse march that added to our musical vocabulary. The title itself, 'Seventy-Six Trombones' at once became a part of the language. He could write love songs, comedy songs, patter songs, barbershop quartet songs, all of them of the top-rank. And he could tell a story." Freeman's column was published on June 23, 2000. This is the same Don Freeman, writing for the same newspaper, who wrote on March 2, 1958: "Willson's music, in short, stands apart as something special and, quite likely, something very durable. . . . Now then, forgetting sentiment, I suggest that 'Seventy-Six Trombones' exudes all the fire and bounce and joy, all the sheer rhythmic sock—and all of the greatness of "Alexander's Ragtime Band." He could not have been more prescient.

Across the continent from San Diego, Jay Nordlinger, managing editor of *National Review*, wrote in June 2000 that "Willson had one masterpiece in him and it will live as long as there is anything like musical theater. *The Music Man* is an astonishing creation. It came in a spurt of brilliance. It is shot through with originality, verve—and, why not go all the way—genius." Nordlinger pointed out that at every opportunity in the show, music is exalted—through the con man, the piano teacher, the piano student, the librarian, the barbershop quartet, and, of course, the prospect of having a boy's band.

Thousands of miles from San Diego and New York, in the little town of Benson in northwest Minnesota, Dr. R. Galen Hanson, a retired professor who holds a Ph.D. in sociology, claims *The Music Man* may be the best story of a small town ever written. Never have small-town values and attitudes been better portrayed than what Willson achieved in *The Music Man,* he says. The charm and the longevity of *The Music Man*, contends Hanson, stretch far beyond its music.

> He had the boy in the wheelchair in his first draft and changed it to the boy with the lisp. But almost every character in *The Music Man* is crippled in some way. Harold Hill is the flawed con man. Marian is the prude who's never been in love. Mayor Shinn is pompous, and his wife is a bore. Even the school board members say they haven't gotten along in 20 years. Everybody comes with their disability. The only thing that can help them is love. There have been all sorts of sociological studies done on life in small towns, dozens of them. I've participated in some. There's never been a better study of small-town life than what Meredith Willson did in *The Music Man*.

Dr. Hanson, who co-authored a book entitled, *Small Town and the Nation: The Conflict of Local and Translocal Forces*, explains how the same basic theme shows up in all of Willson's work. "It is someone bringing an uplifting message of hope, the transformative power of love as a healing potion, the only real healer in all of the world. It is shown in Winthrop, the little boy with the lisp. Professor Harold Hill brought him new life and hope, music to his soul. Mayor Shinn and Eulalie Shinn get new life; they change, mellow before your eyes from strict rigidity to caring and warm."

Hanson believes Willson's early work with Charlie Chaplin influenced his use of symbols on stage to make his point. One of the most telling moments in *The Music Man*, he claims, is when Professor Hill stands on the footbridge and, while waiting for Marian, breaks a seemingly insignificant stick.

> He breaks the twig on the footbridge and he, in his deepest interior self, has made a commitment. In all true love, there is a break from the past self in the lover. In all great moments of the human heart, there are many—not merely a few—things going on while feelings are being felt. And we go through process steps to get to true love. The writer, musician, composer, storyteller Willson knows about this very delicate process of steps—sometimes two forward, one backward—to true love and gives us here, with Hill directing with a twig, a symbol of the eternal process—steps all people feel. For at one moment, he stands up very sharply and confidently, as if, with twig in hand, a maestro directing not merely a band but an orchestra. This gesture—directing the orchestra with a twig—is still professor (salesman, con artist). But then—then—in an especially extraordinary moment, Harold breaks the twig and throws it away—and by throwing away the symbol of his fraud, he is now, and more powerfully, a man whose heart is filled no longer with manipulation but with true love.

In demonstrating what Hanson believes to be Willson's genius, he compares the scene with the twig on the footbridge with Marian's stirring defense of Professor Hill to the townspeople. "Marian takes a pointer from the blackboard, breaks it off and hands it to Hill for a baton to lead the band. As Hill broke a twig on the footbridge when they fell in love, now Marian breaks a twig (the classroom pointer) and puts it back, with love, into his hands. And there is music," adds Dr. Hanson.

The same theme crops up in most of Willson's other works, he explains:

> Leadville Johnny and Molly Brown bring elements of much needed warmth (love) to the 'upper crust' of the city of Denver. Love also lifted them. Life is more than wearing our social class name tags too proudly.
>
> In *Here's Love*, Santa, on trial, gains testimony from the people whose lives have been lifted by love (through Santa). We *need* a little Christmas (like food and water) to survive and thrive.
>
> There is a social realism and momentary misjudging in many of the elements of the Willson body of work—that is, the world does not automatically receive this saving, uplifting love. It brings with it resistance and obstacles.
>
> Professor Hill meets the resistance and faces serious legal repercussions (trial and tribulation). Marian's loving defense speech, in Hill's behalf, is Willson's hymn to love's uplifting power. Santa Claus in *Here's Love* faces trial and tribulation, too. Willson's reply: We need a little Christmas. Molly Brown and husband are shunned

and ostracized until once again, in Willson's music, love triumphs in the end.

This is a massive legacy because Willson has restated for us one of the lasting truths even befitting of a technological age (maybe more than ever befitting of a cold, technological world): the healing, transformative and profound uplifting power of love.

Dr. Hanson believes that one lyric in the beloved "May the Good Lord Bless and Keep You" epitomizes what Willson says over and over again through the many songs he wrote for his characters: "May the Good Lord bless and keep you—never mind what might have been . . ." That, said Hanson, is the essence of breaking the twig. "If music, stories and art can move and inspire people once in history, there is a real chance that they may once again—years or decades or centuries later. This is when an art form becomes immortal. I believe Willson's works move and inspire us post- moderns now, I also believe they will move and inspire into far-off futures as well. Thereby, Willson's body of work, lyrics, stories and musicianship will be, is now already immortal in the best sense of the word."

Hanson met Meredith and Rini Willson in 1961 when he was an undergraduate at Southern Methodist University in Dallas. "I was a senior at SMU. Meredith and Rini were giving a concert. I was working backstage, so during the show, I sat on a chair about 10 feet behind the curtain," he said. "Meredith had 5,000 in the auditorium that night, many of them stuffy academic types who were likely to sit on their hands all night. He made them get up and sing, 'May the Good Lord Bless and Keep You,' and from that point on, he had them."

Willson and *The Music Man* left a lasting impression on the young student. "To me," he remembers, "it is the classic story of the redemption of a womanizer, a guy who has a girl in every town but who has never been in love and a girl who is just the opposite, someone with abstract dreams but who has never even been on a date. Think about it," he adds. "They both came a million miles to meet on the footbridge that night."

After the show in Dallas, Willson gave Hanson his autograph with a bit of advice thrown in for good measure: "Leave them with something they didn't have when they came."

As Hanson sees it, "Satisfying another human being was the most important thing to him—more important than money. In terms of charisma, I'd rate him right up there with John F. Kennedy and Hubert Humphrey. There never was an absence of Mason City in that man's soul. That really came out loud and clear in him."

Think of it this way, he added, "Hardly anyone knows that Henry Kissinger was from Brooklyn or that Richard Nixon was from Everywhere—but Meredith Willson, from Mason City, Iowa, still works."

Sculptor Clifford Carlson walked around the Euchre and Cycle Club at the Hotel Hanford in 1962, trying to get just the right angle, trying to capture the essence of the jovial personality with the dark horn-rimmed glasses playing the piano. His was no small task.

Carlson was a sculptor, and he was going to craft into clay the spirit of a man who had played with Sousa and Toscanini, experimented with Dr. Lee deForest, written more than 400 songs, including three number one hits

Meredith Willson relaxes with friends in the Hotel Hanford in Mason City after the premiere of *The Music Man*. To his right are Shirley Jones, director Morton Da Costa (holding eight-year-old Ronnie Howard) and Robert Preston. MCPLA

and two symphonies, and had one of the most recognized names in radio because he had taken the professional risk of allowing himself to be both a musician and a stooge for comedians.

When the song ended, the throng of stars and locals clapped and laughed, inspiring the performer to stretch his fingers yet again over the white and black keys of the Hanford's grand piano. The musician sitting a few feet from Carlson was at the peak of his career as the composer of one of the greatest Broadway musicals of all time.

Perhaps the essence of the man, the way he would most want to be remembered, is as Dr. Hanson put it: Meredith Willson, from Mason City, Iowa, still works."

Appendix 1

Spare Type

❑ Willson received five honorary doctorate degrees, the only degrees he ever received after high school.

❑ In the movie *The Shootist*, starring John Wayne, scenes are shot on the main street in town. The "town" set is the same one that was used in *The Music Man*.

❑ One of the stars of *The Shootist* was Ron Howard, who also appeared in *The Music Man*.

❑ In June 1980, Willson attended a performance of *The Music Man* put on by Beverly Hills High School. One of the actors was Patrick Cassidy, son of Shirley Jones, who starred in *The Music Man* movie.

❑ In the 1960 movie *The Apartment* starring Jack Lemmon and Shirley McLaine, there is a scene in which McLaine stands up Lemmon for a date they had. They had made plans to see *The Music Man* on Broadway.

❑ Robert Preston's next movie after *The Music Man* was *How the West Was Won,* which also starred Debbie Reynolds, who had starred in *The Unsinkable Molly Brown.*

❑ Most Americans are familiar with Willson's "It's Beginning to Look A Lot Like Christmas" and think it's the title of the song. It isn't. The title is simply "It's Beginning to Look Like Christma*s*"—without the "a lot."

❑ Forrest Tucker played Professor Harold Hill in the first road show of *The Music Man*. He always figured the role was made for him because he was born in Indiana, the "birthplace" of Professor Hill.

❏   Dick Van Dyke played Harold Hill in the first Broadway revival of *The Music Man.*

❏   In *The Music Man* movie, Professor Harold Hill was coming to River City from Brighton, Illinois. In the play, it's Rock Island, Illinois. One possible reason for the change—Brighton was Willson's mother's home town. He probably snuck it into the script as a subtle tribute to her.

❏   Willson wrote three autobiographical books: *There I Stood With My Piccolo, Eggs I Have Laid,* and *"You Gotta Know The Territory."* He had an idea for a fourth one, *Everybody's a Name Dropper—Particularly Me* but he never finished it.

❏   Willson wrote one novel entitled *Look What They Did to Fedalia.*

❏   In 1964, the Beatles made their American television debut on the Ed Sullivan television show. They sang five songs. One of them was Willson's "Till There Was You."

❏   The following performers—The Andrews Sisters, Bing Crosby, Eddie Arnold, Gene Autry, Pat Boone, Frankie Laine, Johnny Mathis, Jim Nabors, Boots Randolph, Jim Reeves, Roy Rogers, Kate Smith and Tammy Wynette all recorded or did public performances in which they sang, "May The Good Lord Bless and Keep You."

❏   Willson donated some of his memorabilia to UCLA. A few years later, on a visit to the university, he stopped at the music department and asked if he could see how his material was displayed. No one knew what he was talking about. After several minutes of scurrying around, the Willson donations were located—stuffed away in a closet.

Awards and Honors

1941: Academy Award nomination, original score, *The Great Dictator.*
1942: Academy Award nomination, original score, *The Little Foxes.*
1953: Honorary degree, doctor of music, Parsons College
1958: New York Drama Circle Award, best musical, *The Music Man.*
1958: Tony Award, best musical, *The Music Man.*
1958: Outer Circle Award, best new musical, *The Music Man.*
1959: Honorary degree, doctor of music, Coe College.
1959: Grammy Award, best Broadway original cast album, *The Music Man.*
1960: NARAS award nomination, best show album, original cast, *The Unsinkable Molly Brown.*
1960: United States Army Certificate of Appreciation for patriotic civilian service.
1961: Humanitarian Award as "Big Brother of the Year," presented by President John F. Kennedy.
1962: Golden Globe Award, best motion picture musical, *The Music Man.*
1963: Gold record, in recognition of 1 million album sales, *The Music Man.*
1963: Screen Writers Award, best written American musical, *The Music Man.*
1963: NARAS nomination, best original score from show album, *Here's Love.*
1963: Honorary degree, doctor of literature, Indiana Institute of Technology.
1963: Distinguished Service Award, University of Iowa.

1966: National Council of the Humanities membership, appointed by President Lyndon B. Johnson.

1973: Honorary degree, doctor of fine arts, Regis College.

1976: Americanism Parade Bicentennial Award, parade grand marshal, Americanism Parade.

1979: Honorary degree, doctor of music, Wartburg College.

1982: Elected to Songwriters Hall of Fame by National Academy of Popular Music.

1988: Presidential Medal of Freedom, presented posthumously by President Ronald Reagan.

1988: Iowa Award for lifetime achievement (given once every five years) presented posthumously by Gov. Terry Branstad.

1999: Meredith Willson commemorative postage stamp issued.

The Music Man

The stage production

Produced by Kermit Bloomgarden with Herbert Greene in association with Frank Productions Inc.; directed by Morton DaCosta; opened at the Majestic Theatre on Broadway on Dec. 19, 1957 and ran for 1,375 performances.

The Cast (in order of appearance):

Traveling salesmen: Russell Goodwin, Hal Norman, Robert Howard, James Gannon, Robert Lenn, Vernon Lusby, Robert Evans.

CHARLIE COWELL: Paul Reed
CONDUCTOR: Carl Nicholas
HAROLD HILL: Robert Preston
MAYOR SHINN: David Burns
BUFFALO BILLS: Al Shea, Wayne Ward, Vern Reed, Bill Spangenberg
MARCELLUS WASHBURN: Iggy Wolfington
TOMMY: Danny Carroll
MARIAN PAROO: Barbara Cook
MRS. PAROO: Pert Kelton
AMARYLLLIS: Marilyn Siegel

WINTHROP PAROO: Eddie Hodges
EULALIE MACKENZIE SHINN: Helen Raymond
ZANEETA SHINN: Dusty Worrall
GRACIE SHINN: Barbara Travis
ALMA HIX: Adnia Rice
MAUDE DUNLAP: Elaine Swann
ETHEL TOFFELMIER: Peggy Mondo
MRS. SQUIRES: Martha Flynn
CONSTABLE LOCKE: Carl Nicholas

The National Company

Produced by Kermit Bloomgarden with Herbert Greene in association with Frank Productions Inc.; directed by Morton DaCosta; opened at the Philharmonic Auditorium in Los Angeles on Aug, 18, 1958.

The Cast (in order of appearance):

Traveling salesmen: Lewis Bolyard, Walter Kelvin, Lou Polacek, Richard Fredricks, Rudy Jenkins, Jimy Weis and Charles Karel

CHARLIE COWELL: Harry Hickox
CONDUCTOR: Earl George
HAROLD HILL: Robert Preston
MAYOR SHINN: Cliff Hall
FRISCO FOUR: Byron Mellberg, James Ingram, Jay F. Smith, Allan Louw
MARCELLUS WASHBURN: Benny Baker
TOMMY: Robert Piper
MARIAN PAROO: Joan Weldon
MRS. PAROO: Lucie Lancaster
AMARYLLLIS: Kay Cole
WINTHROP PAROO: Lynn Potter
EULALIE MACKENZIE SHINN: Carol Veazie
ZANEETA SHINN: Susan Luckey
GRACIE SHINN: Jan Tanzy
ALMA HIX: Jean Bruno
MAUDE DUNLAP: Mary Alice Wunderle
ETHEL TOFFELMIER: Lu Leonard
MRS. SQUIRES: Marceline Decker
CONSTABLE LOCKE: Earl George

The Movie

Produced by Morton DaCosta with Joel Freeman in association with Warner Brothers; directed by Morton DaCosta; released in 1962.

The Cast (in order of appearance):

Traveling salesmen: Russell Goodwin, Hal Norman, Robert Howard, James Gannon, Robert Lenn, Vernon Lusby, Robert Evans.

CHARLIE COWELL: Henry Hickox
CONDUCTOR: Percy Helton
HAROLD HILL: Robert Preston
MAYOR SHINN: Paul Ford
BUFFALO BILLS: Al Shea, Wayne Ward, Vern Reed, Bill Spangenberg
MARCELLUS WASHBURN: Buddy Hackett
TIMMY: Tommy Djilas
MARIAN PAROO: Shirley Jones
MRS. PAROO: Pert Kelton
AMARYLLLIS: Monique Vermont
WINTHROP PAROO: Ronnie Howard
EULALIE MACKENZIE SHINN: Hermione Gingold
ZANEETA SHINN: Susan Luckey
GRACIE SHINN: Barbara Travis
ALMA HIX: Adnia Rice
MAUDE DUNLAP: Sara Seegar
ETHEL TOFFELMIER: Peggy Mondo
MRS. SQUIRES: Mary Wickes
CONSTABLE LOCKE: Charles Lane
JESSLYN FAX: Avis Grubb

Appendix 4

The Books and Music
of Meredith Willson

Books

What Every Young Musician Should Know
And There I Stood With My Piccolo
Eggs I Have Laid
Look What They Did to Fedalia (fiction)
You Gotta Know the Territory

Symphonies

Symphony No. 1 in F-Minor: A Symphony of San Francisco
Missions of California

Songs

Afraid
Alabama Christmas
America Calling
An American Anthem
The American Legion March
Anaconda Copper
And Still the Volga Flows
And That is That
And There I Stood With My Piccolo
Answer Me
Answer the Call
Anthem of the Atomic Age
Are You Sure?
Arkansas
Arm in Arm
Ask Not
At the Junction of the Chenango
    and the Susou
La Baie Verte
Band
Banners and Bonnets
Beautiful People of Denver
Being in Love
Belly Up to the Bar, Boys
Big Clown Balloons
The Big Show
Bill
Blow
Blue Ridge Mountains
Blue Ridge Mountains of North
    Carolina
Bluestem Bowl
Bon Jour (The Language Song)
Bowbells
Boy Meets Girl
British Grenadiers
Buffalo Fight Song
Bugle
Cabadaster
Cadence

Cadenza
Calico Square Dance
The California Story
Canada Dry Water
Centennial
Cherokee Kid
Chestnut Street
Chick a Pen
Chicken Fat
A Child's Letter
Chords
Christmas Presents
Chuck Wagon Gang
Chuckle a Day
The City
Colorado My Home
Colorado Sunset
Complaint Fanfare
Complexities of Radio
Country Tune
Cow Ponies Always Weep
Crypto Vestimenta
Dear Mr. Santa Claus
Deck the Halls
Defiance
The Denver Police
Derry Up, Derry Down
Dining Car
Do Sol Do
Dolce Far Niente
Don't Put Bananas On
Doors of the World Swing on New
    Britain Hinge
Dosi Dos
Dream Along
Dynamite Blasting
Eat, Drink and Be Healthy
Encore Suite
Everybody Knows Everybody
Every Day

Expect Things to Happen
Falling Star
Fan Mail
Fedalia
Fiddle Iddle Up
Fillamaroo
Finagle
Finale
Finale (Here's Love)
Finale (*The Unsinkable Molly
    Brown*)
Fire Up
The First One
Florida
Florida Oranges
For a Song
For I for S Forever
Fords Out Front
Forth and Back
The Fourth
The Freedom Song
G Minor is My Favorite Key
Gangway, You Rats, Gangway
Gary, Indiana
Gay Friends Are Essential
Gentle and Sentimental
Gentleman Tramp
George
Gold Rush Towns
Gone to Chicago
Goodnight Ladies
Goodnight My Darling
Goodnight My Someone
Gracie
The Great Dictator
Green Bay Wisconsin
Haffner
Happy Birthday, Mrs. J. J. Brown
Happy Go Lucky
Happy, Happy, Happy, Happy
He's My Friend
Heart Fund Valentine
Here Comes the Queen
Here Comes the Springtime

Here's a Song Everyone Can Sing
Here's Love
Hi Lee, Hi Low
Hit the Leather
Horse Sense
House of Melody
Husband
I Ain't Down Yet
I'd Like a Memory
I Got News
I Know It and You Know It
I Know Why
I'll Never Say Good Bye to You
    Again
I'll Never Say No
I'll Sing No Duet With You
I May Never Fall in Love With You
I Never Thought I'd Be Along Here
I See the Moon
I Take a Dim View
I Take Just as Pride in My Dear
    Little Bride
I've Already Started In
I Want to Go to Chicago
If I Knew
If There Were No Men in the World
If There Were No Women at All
If You Don't Mind My Saying
Ignore Dior
Indian Music
Iowa
Iowa Fight Song
Iowa Indian Song
Iowa Stubborn
It is G, It is Minor, It's Mozart
It's Beginning to Look Like
    Christmas
It's Easter Time
It's Good For You
It's Half Past Kissin'
It's You
Jamboree
Jello Shimmer
Josephine

Just Becuz
Just Like Song
Just Like a Woman
Ke Toky I O
Keep a Hoppin'
Kiss the Girls Good Morning
The Last Word
Laura Lee
The Lawn Mower Waltz
Leadville Johnny Brown
Let Freedom Ring
Lida Rose
Lift Up Your Voice
Little Foxes
Little Hours Music
Local Boy Makes Good
Look Little Girl, Here's Love
Loud and Soft
Love, Come Take Me Again
Magic Valley
Mail Call March
Marching to Pretoria
Marguerite Waltz
Marian the Librarian
La Marseillaise
Mason City, Go
May The Good Lord Bless and Keep
   You
The Melody Man
Memories I'll Never Forget
Meredith Willson's March
Mind If I Tell You I Love You
Missions of California
Moon, Moon
Mother Darlin
The Mule
Music Across the Waters
My Grandmother's
My Little Bird
My Own Brass Bed
My Signature
My State of Kansas, My Home
My Ten Ton Baby and Me
My White Knight

My Wish
Never Feel Too Weary to Pray
Now We Sing
Number Four
Nylons
Occupancy of This Building is
   Limited to 382
Oh I Wanna Go
Oh What a Wonderful Song
Oh Where Can There Be
Oh Where Oh Where
Old Jello Theme
On The Big Red Letter
Original Music
Our Home Town
Overture from *The Music Man*
Overture from *Here's Love*
Overture from *The Unsinkable
   Molly Brown*
Palmy Pinellas Peninsula
Parade Fantastique
Peony Bush
Phenomena
Pi Phi Sweetheart
Piano Lesson
Piccolo Polka
Pick a Little, Talk a Little
Pine Cones and Holly Berries
Plastic Alligator
Politely
Polonaise Militaire
The Postman
Postmas Visits the Burns
Practice Makes Perfect
Precipite Volissime Volmente
Queen
Radio City Suite
Rakoczy March
Remember Hawaii
Remington Rollmatic March
Revenge Music
Robert Schumann
Rock Island Rock
Rosalie

Rovin' and Dreamin'
Running Water
Sadder But Wiser Girl
The Same Little Chapel
San Diego Waltz
San Juan Bautista
San Juan Capistrano
The Scherzo
Scotland The Brave
Sequence
Seventy-Six Trombones
Share The Luck
She Hadda Go Back
Shipoopi
Sincere
Sing Fiddle Sing
Smile With Me
Sneezing Violins
Song of Steel
Spindletop
Summer Breeze Song
Symphonic Variations
Symphony of San Francisco
Tapioca Polka
Texaco Star Parade
That Man Over There
Thingumamobs
Thirty Two Bars of I Love You
This Concerto Has It
This is It
This is Haffner
This is The Song
Thoughts While Strolling
Three Chimes of Silver
Three Ways
Till There Was You
Timbuctoo
Timpanogos Glacier
To Shorten or Not to Shorten
Toodelso
Toot a Loor
Tornado
The Tuscarora
Two Famous Words

Two in Love
Unsinkable Molly Brown
Up Where The Joke's Going On
Very Giacoso
Waukegan Was a Thriving and
    Prosperous City
We're Going to Schenectady
We're Spending Our Honeymoon
    in Escrow
Wells Fargo Wagon
When the Circus Wagon Came to
    Town
Where's The Third One?
Who Needs What Moonlight?
Whose Dream Are You?
Will I Ever Tell You
Will The Passengers
Willson Tag
WIN
Wings on High
Wisconsin Cheese
The World Famous Horseshoe
    Curve
The World's Your Oyster
Ya Got Trouble
Yankee Doodle
Yankee Doodle Girl
You and I
You Can't Have a Show
You Don't Know
You'll Love the Singing
You Will Hear it Soon

The Music Man Square

*T*he Music Man Square is about music, fun, and nostalgia. Now under construction, this multi-million dollar complex is located in Mason City Iowa—Meredith's hometown and his model for River City, the town portrayed in *The Music Man*. Thousands of Willson fans recently witnessed the initial dedication ceremony of the Square.

When complete, the Square will feature: (1) The Exploratorium, designed to interest children in instrumental music; (2) A 1912 River City Streetscape, with such landmarks as the Pleazol Pool Hall, a barbershop, soda fountain, and Mrs. Paroo's Front Porch, and will incorporate set designs from the Warner Brothers motion picture; (3) The Museum, a collection of Meredith Willson memorabilia; (4) A music conservancy for persons of all ages and levels of accomplishments; (5) a 500-seat Mason City Community Theater; (6) The Reunion Hall; and (7) The Meredith Willson Boyhood Home, which the foundation has purchased, restored, and incorporated into The Music Man Square.

None of this would have been possible without the generous assistance of Rosemary Willson, Meredith's widow. In 1996, Rosemary offered to match, up to $5,000,000, every dollar raised by the Foundation for this worthwhile cultural project, plus a $2,000,000 Endowment Fund. The 1912

(Right): The restored
and now open Meredith
Willson Boyhood Home;
(Below) A rendition of
The Music Man Square.
Both are located in
Mason City, Iowa, and
are operated by The
Mason City Foundation.

Streetscape will be dedicated in 2001, and on May 18, 2002—Meredith Willson's 100th birthday and the 40th anniversary of *The Music Man* movie—the Grand Opening will be held!

The Square is on schedule and on target. We encourage your support, and welcome donations. Our mailing address is: The Mason City Foundation, 208 East State Street, Box 518, Mason City, IA 50401-0518. You may contact us directly at 641-421-7893 (phone); musicman@mach3ww.com (e-mail); or www.themusicmansquare.org (web site address).

Thank you for your support. Please visit us soon.

Carl R. Miller
Executive Director
The Mason City Foundation

Bibliography

Manuscript Sources

The papers of W. Earl Hall, University of Iowa Archives, Iowa City, Iowa
Miscellaneous papers, Mason City Foundation Archives, Mason City, Iowa
Miscellaneous papers, Mason City Public Library Archives, Mason City, Iowa

Books

Blythe, Cheryl and Susan Sackett. *Say Goodnight, Gracie: The Story of Burns & Allen.* New York: E.P. Dutton Co., 1986.

Brooks, Tim and Earle Marsh. *The Complete Directory to Prime Time Network and Cable TV Shows.* New York: Ballantine Books, 1995.

Buxton, Frank and Bill Owen. *The Big Broadcast: 1920-1950.* New York: The Hearst Co., 1972.

McNeil, Alex. *Total Television Including Cable.* New York: Penguin Books, 1991.

Morrow, Lee Allen. *The Tony Award Book.* New York: Abbeville Press, 1987.

Nachman, Gerald. *Raised on Radio.* New York: Random House, 1998.

Robinson, David. *Chaplin: His Life and Art.* New York: McGraw-Hill Book Co., 1985.

Sheward, David. *It's a Hit.* New York: WatsonGuptill Publications, 1994.

Slate, Sam J. and Joe Cook. *It Sounds Impossible.* New York: The MacMillan Co., 1963.

Willson, Meredith. *What Every Young Musician Should Know.* New York: Robbins, 1938.

——. *And There I Stood With My Piccolo.* New York: Doubleday, 1948.

——. *Eggs I Have Laid.* New York: Henry Holt and Co., 1955.

——. *But He Doesn't Know the Territory.* New York, G.P. Putnam's Sons, 1959.

Newspapers

Asbury Park (N.J.) *Evening Press,* July 11, 1964

Cedar Rapids Gazette, November 16, 1980

Chicago Sun-Times, April 12, 1938

Christian Science Monitor, February 26, 1951

Columbia (S.C.) *State,* February 1, 1958

Des Moines Register, August 21, 1923; Dec. 24, 1930; October 19, 1940; March 5, 1947

Detroit Free-Press, August 14, 1963

Hollywood Citizen-News, March 13, 1948

Hollywood Reporter, September 4, 1969

Los Angeles Daily News, November 15, 1951

Los Angeles Times, September 4, 1969; June 16, 1984

Mason City (IA) *Times,* May 4, 1915; Nov. 24, 1916

Mason City (IA) *Globe-Gazette,* November 21, 1923; September 3, 1926; June 15, 1928; September 14, 1931; June 3, 1936; March 29, 1938; December 3, 1940; March 8, 1941; August 30, 1941; Jan. 31, 1944; Dec. 20, 1944; Aug. 7, 1945; September 30, 1946; February 17, 1948; March 19, 1948; March 3, 1953; December 12, 1953; March 17, 1958; June 6, 1958; June 12, 1958; July 21, 1958; April 4, 1960; November 5, 1960; July 28, 1962; October 16, 1962; August 10, 1963; Sept. 18, 1963; Feb. 27, 1964; June 5, 1964; June 8, 1964; January 24, 1966; July 11, 1968; March 18, 1972; February 7, 1974; February 9, 1974; January 14, 1975; June 1, 1976; June 11, 1976; July 14, 1979; June 16, 1984; June 17, 1984; June 18, 1984; June 19, 1984; June 20, 1984; June 21, 1984; June 22, 1984; January 29, 2000

Musical Express, August 31, 1951

New York Daily News, Nov. 10, 1951; Dec. 20, 1957; January 12, 1958; March 31, 1964

New York Herald-Tribune, December 15, 1957; Dec. 20, 1957

New York Journal-American, December 20, 1957

New York Times, September 24, 1951; December 20, 1957; Sept. 4, 1969; June 16, 1984

New York World Telegram and Sun, December 20, 1957

Norwalk (CT) *Sentinel,* April 14, 1938

Orlando Sentinel, April 18, 1992

San Diego Union, March 2, 1958; May 31, 1993; June 23, 2000; July 21, 2000

San Francisco Chronicle, April 12, 1936; April 17, 1936; April 20, 1936; Aug. 2, 1936;

Seattle Times, June 5, 1929

St. Louis Post Dispatch, December 28, 1979

St. Louis Star-Tribune, April 4, 1938

Variety, April 11, 1962

Magazines

Klein, Jerry, "Meet the Music Man," *Family Weekly*, June 8, 1958

"Meredith Willson: Sextuple-Threat Man," *Doubleday Magazine*, February 1952

"New Musical in Manhattan," *Time*, Dec. 30, 1957

"Products Make a Broadway Hit," *Chicago Tribune Magazine*, April 20, 1958

"New Musical on Broadway," *Time*, Nov. 14, 1960

"It Shouldn't Happen to Santa Claus," *Time*, Oct. 11, 1963

Oates, William, "America's Music Man: Meredith Willson," *Nostalgia Digest*, August-September 1994

"Products Make a Broadway Hit," *Chicago Tribune Magazine*, April 20, 1958

"Good Pickings," *Time*, April 21, 1958

Willson, Dixie, "The Man Behind The Music Man," *American Weekly*, May 4, 1958

"*You and I*," *Super Song Book*, April 1941

"*Willson Says Writing Anything Painful Chore*," *Capitol News*, December 1951

Nordlinger, Jay, "One Vote for Willson," *National Review*, June 5, 2000.

Broadcasts

"Good News," National Broadcasting Company, June 29, 1939

"Command Performance," Armed Forces Radio Service, Feb. 15, 1945

"George Burns and Gracie Allen," National Broadcasting Company, Jan. 17, 1946

"Hallmark Radio Playhouse," National Broadcasting Company, March 10, 1949

"The Big Show," National Broadcasting Company, March 9, 1952

"Interview with Rosemary Willson," KGLO Radio, June 1, 1994

Index

About the Author:

John C. Skipper is a newspaper journalist whose 35-year career has produced thousands of newspaper columns and five books, including *Umpires: Classic Baseball Stories from the Men Who Made the Calls* and *A Biographical Dictionary of the Baseball Hall of Fame* (McFarland). John and his wife Sandi live in Mason City, Iowa. They have three grown daughters and one grandchild.